Liberty,
Dicta & Force

Louis E. Carabini
4910 Birch Street
Newport Beach, CA 92660
louc2@cox.net
Audio Version: store.mises.org

*To all those minding their own business
while tending to my every need.*

Liberty, Dicta & Force

Why Liberty Brings Out the Best in People and How Government Brings Out the Worst

LOUIS E. CARABINI

MISESINSTITUTE

AUBURN, ALABAMA

Mises Institute
518 West Magnolia Ave.
Auburn, Ala. 36832
mises.org

paperback edition: 978-1-61016-693-5
epub edition: 978-1-61016-695-9

Contents

Introduction

IN THE SUMMER OF 1961, I was returning from a fishing trip with my friend George Vermillion. We were both in our early thirties. George was a pharmacist and I worked for Parke Davis, a pharmaceutical company. We had been fishing in Mexico, and George was driving us back home to Long Beach, California — a trip that would take about three hours. During the drive, I told him (it was more like a confession) I had never registered to vote and was embarrassed about not knowing the difference between a Democrat and a Republican. I thought it was time I learned about politics and joined the crowd, but most of all I wanted to avoid embarrassment when questioned about my political affiliation.

My main interest outside of family affairs was science; politics and economics were too esoteric for my taste. Other than the required courses, my classes in college were in the biological sciences. George was the perfect person to ask about politics, given that his father, George "Red" Vermillion, a Democrat, had been the mayor of Long Beach from 1954 to 1957 and his mother was the president of the Long Beach Republican Club. Imagine growing up in that household! So, George began explaining things to me. He talked nonstop for well over an hour, and I don't recall

asking any questions along the way. When he finished, I
told him I should become a Republican because personal
responsibility and free enterprise struck a chord with me. I
felt relieved that I could now at least call myself something:
a Republican. (I should mention George was a Republican;
it seems his mother got the best of him.)

A few weeks later, George invited me to a meeting
where Assemblyman Joe Shell was speaking about his campaign against Richard Nixon in the California Republican
gubernatorial primary race. I went to the meeting where
there were twenty or thirty people in attendance. As Shell
spoke about what he would do if he were elected governor, he touched upon some of the same thoughts George
had expressed to me during our trip. After he spoke, he
took time to meet with each of us. When he got to me, he
asked where I lived. When I told him, he asked if I would
be willing to run his campaign in that part of Orange
County. I gulped and said yes. Within minutes, a newspaper reporter and photographer had me shaking hands with
Joe, flanked by the California and US flags. That was my
introduction to politics, of which I still knew next to nothing. The following day, the picture was in a local newspaper. How proud could I be? Just a few weeks earlier,
I hadn't known the difference between a Democrat and a
Republican, and now I was running a local campaign for
a conservative Republican. No sooner had I escaped one
embarrassment than I found myself right back in another.
I didn't have a clue about what to do as a local campaign
manager. I was on a crash course to learn about what it
meant to be not just a Republican, but a *conservative* one.

As a local campaign manager, I had to recruit workers and try to woo voters to our side. Recruiting workers
was easy because I only solicited people who already considered themselves conservative Republicans. Most were
around my age, and getting together with like-minded
people who shared a common agenda — with dinners and
cocktail parties thrown in — was a fun and stimulating
experience. In the process, I learned from my recruits, who

had already read many conservative books and essays, which they either gave me or told me about. After doing some reading and becoming somewhat comfortable with my newly gained knowledge, I was ready to spread the word and persuade voters.

Because the internet and PCs were not yet available, all campaign materials were in print form. We simply delivered the literature door to door. I even commandeered my two sons — ages five and seven at the time — to fill their wagon with literature, which they distributed in the neighborhood. They eventually got to know by precinct number where their friends lived. The campaign went well, with hopes of an upset. However, when the final votes were counted in June 1962, Shell had lost to Nixon, 35 percent to 65 percent. Over the next two years, I became involved in various other conservative Republican campaigns and, in the process, achieved a perfect record of zero to whatever.

At some point while campaigning, someone asked me a question that put me on a different course: "If your free enterprise system is so great, then what about schools, roads, laws, and justice?" I don't remember my answer, but that question was just too simple and fundamental for me not to have considered it when I first got involved in politics. I would like to think the question was at the back of my mind from the beginning and that I had just hoped no one would ask. More likely, though, I had feared the answers might cause me to doubt, or even reject, the efficacy of free markets. Nevertheless, there I stood, shifting from where I was a few months earlier when I had wondered, "What is the difference between a Republican and a Democrat?" to now wondering, "Is there a difference?" After all, neither party suggested that markets free of government intervention would be able to provide all goods and services more effectively than politically regulated markets could.

Why would nature's feedback favor the efficacy of free markets for some enterprises and not others? If nature's feedback favored the efficacy of free (politically unrestricted) enterprises A, B, and C, why would it disfavor the efficacy of free enterprises X, Y, and Z, unless there was something peculiar or unique about them? If a free, unrestricted market was capable of delivering fresh milk to my front door, as was the case when I was a kid, it would seem natural that such a market would also be capable of delivering mail to my front door if allowed to do so, which was and is still not the case. But then, maybe both enterprises would fare better as government-regulated markets.

For nature to be inconsistent seemed implausible. Either a free market is a more efficacious social arrangement than a politically restricted market for all enterprises or no enterprises. Double standards seemed unnatural. I simply adopted the free-market alternative as more universally efficacious because my inherent bias drew me there, which was reinforced by the concern that if regulated markets did lead to greater efficiency and productivity, such would hold true for the most minute market exchanges.

In addition to my free-market bias, I regarded my life as my sole responsibility. Partial responsibility in which others become responsible for part of my life and I responsible for part of theirs was incomprehensible.

Around 1962, the Foundation for Economic Education (FEE) came to my attention with its published collection *Clichés of Socialism*. The collection consisted of a couple dozen or so essays printed on 8½ x 11 inch sheets, each on a socialist cliché. The essays described the failures of socialist policies and the fallacious reasoning behind the clichés. Although I was excited to find some justification for free markets, the responses to these clichés did not tell me *why* free markets work better or even why socialism doesn't work. Nonetheless, *Clichés of Socialism* and other FEE materials led me to books and essays that kept my search alive. Discovering the *why* obviates the need to analyze every enterprise by every group of actors in every part of the world at every given time. Scientific truths are universal, necessary, and certain. If applying the free market to food production would lead to better food supplies in

Oregon, the same should hold true in Zimbabwe — now, one hundred years from now, or one hundred years ago. There are underlying principles of nature that govern matter in motion, irrespective of the enterprise, actors involved, location of the event, or time of occurrence.

Also around 1962, I learned about the Free Enterprise Institute (FEI), a newly formed, for-profit educational organization headquartered in Los Angeles and directed by Andrew Galambos (1924–97), an astrophysicist. Art Sperry, an anesthesiologist I had met as a Parke Davis representative, organized an FEI course given by Galambos in Long Beach. I signed up for the premier V-100 course, "The Science of Volition," which was conducted in fifteen weekly three-hour sessions. There were about twenty people in attendance, many of whom were physicians. This was exactly what I had been looking for because it offered a scientific approach to markets and society.

The thrust of the course was about applying the scientific method as an effective means to gain knowledge and truth about nature. We learned about scientific discoveries and how scientists at the forefront of those discoveries were often threatened, imprisoned, tortured, or executed when their claims about the workings of the world ran counter to the dicta of the ruling authorities. With time, however, discoveries that contradicted such dicta eventually became the norm, while the fallacious ideas became viewed as backward thinking. The threat of death did not stop the Earth from moving, nor did the house arrest of Galileo or the burning at the stake of Giordano Bruno. Threats might delay the general acceptance of the actual workings of nature, but they cannot stop it. Using force to gain adherence to a belief is itself evidence that the belief is likely fallacious and will eventually be discarded.

"Truth is the daughter of time, not authority," noted Francis Bacon (1561–1626). In 1620, he published *The New Organon*, which outlined a step-by-step method to discover the workings of nature as a way of improving the human condition. This was the birth of modern science, destined to replace our superstitions with observable evidence and inductive reasoning. Today, superstitions that contradict reason and observable evidence continue to linger in the minds of those unwilling to accept the reality of nature. Even when we suspect that a generally held belief is fallacious, we are reluctant to express our doubts for fear of being ridiculed by our peers.

When Galileo (1564–1642) turned his newly made, twenty-power telescope to the moon, he was surprised to see mountains. Church dicta claimed that all celestial bodies were heavenly and therefore perfect spheres orbiting the Earth in perfect circles while the Earth lay still at the center. This geocentric structure of the universe was the generally accepted view for two thousand years.

When Galileo invited Cesare Cremonini (1550–1631), the most renowned philosopher of his time, to look through his telescope and see for himself that the moon had mountains and was not a perfect sphere, he simply refused. Perhaps Cremonini was convinced that it was not possible, or more likely was unwilling to look for fear that if he did see mountains and told others about it, fellow scholars would ridicule him and his standing with Church authorities would be jeopardized. Today, few have heard of Cremonini, who was so famous at one time that his portrait hung on the walls of many European castles. To say there were mountains on the moon and the Earth did not lie motionless at the center of the universe was considered heresy. The populace accepted the Church's teachings given that this view of the universe had existed far too long for it to be wrong. If it were wrong, surely someone would have proven it long ago.

Today, virtually everyone considers the geocentric view absurd. However, very few have arrived at that conviction through personal observation and calculation because that would require far more than what most of us are capable of doing. We simply accept what others tell us when we sense that dissent would make us look foolish among our peers. This natural fear of peer rejection is exemplified in the well-known Hans Christian Andersen tale *The Emperor's New Clothes*. In that story, onlookers, for fear of looking stupid amid their peers, are reluctant to express what they see as the emperor parades down the street showing off his "new clothes" — except for a child, too young to be silenced by peer pressure, who reveals that the emperor is indeed wearing no clothes.

Science simply opens doors to new ideas and views that no one is forced to walk through. There is no final authority to decree a scientific view as "settled." This volitional acceptance or rejection of ideas is the overwhelming strength of science that will continue to whittle away at the common belief that states with their dicta and force can serve a beneficial purpose. Improvements in the human condition will continue to emerge from volitional interactions led by scientific discoveries and new technologies that political dogma may dampen, but never stop.

The FEI V-100 course I took began by establishing two postulates: *All volitional beings live to pursue happiness* and *All moral pursuits of happiness are equally valid*. Underlying the first postulate is the innate driving force of living organisms: *self-interest*. At that time, the monumental work of evolutionary biologists George Williams and William Hamilton confirming the genetic selfish nature of animals had yet to be published. Adam Smith (1723–90) and others had suggested man's selfish nature, but rigorous genetic studies confirming such insights would not appear until later.

If people act in their own self-interest, why would anyone ever act morally or civilly without being forced to do so? This is perhaps the greatest misconception held by those trapped in the political box, wherein selfishness is erroneously understood to be in opposition to morality, cooperation, and social order. Selfishness in fact is the quintessential attribute that leads to cooperation and improvement of the human condition. Without selfishness, morality and cooperation would have no meaning, and life itself would be devoid of value. Selfishness is not, as often characterized, a quantitative attribute subject to degrees, such as *too* selfish or greedy. The indispensable selfish nature of living matter will be discussed in chapter 3.

The implied notion that political authorities are necessary stems from the general belief that humans, if left to their own devices, will give rise to a society of "all against all," as Thomas Hobbes asserted. Hobbes was mistaken, as was James Madison, who claimed, "If men were angels, no government would be necessary." Hobbes and Madison imply by their statements that governments are needed to curtail man's worst behavior; however, in actual practice, governments instead encourage man's worst behavior.

Nature doesn't care about bringing out the best or the worst in people. The feedback that follows our actions guides us to either repeat or avoid certain acts in the pursuit of well-being. Positive feedback leads us toward repetition, while negative feedback leads us away. However, government provides a political safe harbor for the most abhorrent acts committed on its behalf. When acting within this safe harbor, an actor can avoid the personal negative feedback of rejection and injury that he or she would otherwise face when acting outside it. With the full force of the state behind them, the lowest minion can act with impunity. The personal impunity from the most abhorrent conduct is just one example of how government brings out the worst in people.

The win/lose combative nature of the political world encourages uncivil conduct which is accepted as the social norm. Outside that world is a win/win volitional environment wherein civil conduct is encouraged and accepted as the social norm. As will be discussed in chapters 2 and 8, people, for the most part, conduct themselves consistent with the accepted social norm of the arena in which they are operating. A person acting uncivilly (using dicta and force) when in the political arena will revert naturally to civil conduct (using volition) when operating outside that arena.

There have been more than a hundred political parties in the United States throughout its history, with about thirty still active, and there are a few hundred more governing or trying to govern people's lives in virtually every other corner of the world. The bickering between and within these ruling groups only concerns how best to rule their designated subjects, with each political group having as its essential common theme the use of dicta and force to gain obedience.

Political schemes have titles that sound appealing because titles that actually describe what they entail would attract few followers. Communism, socialism, liberalism, and democracy are very humanitarian-sounding political names. They connote community, social interaction, liberty, and self-governance, respectively, with an umbrella of human decency and kindness. However, the actions taken by those involved in such schemes can be as ruthless, brutal, and inhumane as the acts committed by those in schemes carrying names that connote what they actually do. In the convoluted world of politics, those who abhor plunder, wars, and the subjugation of their fellowmen by government, while minding their own business, are labeled dangerous and tyrannical. In the world of politics, the clever use of words can twist the minds of even the most thoughtful person into accepting and endorsing schemes that would otherwise defy their basic sense of decency.

I escaped the political box in 1964, and the views expressed here come from outside the world of politics and government.[1] I invite you to escape that box as well. If you have already done so, I hope you will find further reinforcement here for having made that decision.

The thrust of this book is not about changing public policies, limiting or abolishing government, "fixing"

---

[1] I use the terms "political government," "political democracy," "government," and "state" interchangeably as entities with various names that use dicta and force as their primary means to gain obedience from people residing within their declared geographic dominions.

America, or trying to change the world. Nor is this book about a crisis or the notion that if we don't do something soon, civilization will collapse. I hope to convey an appreciation of liberty as the natural common sense way to view the social world and interact within it. The inherent moral compass that guides our behavior in private matters can serve us just as well in public matters.

While political governments are constructs of disutility that cannot serve a useful social purpose, I consider political intervention to limit or abolish them as counterproductive since such activity endorses the use of dicta and force, which is the very reason political governments are constructs of disutility in the first place. Advancing social ideas that do not demand obedience or compliance requires far more personal patience than simply forcing others to comply via the political ballot box. Nevertheless, by way of volition, the widely held idea that dicta and force can serve a useful purpose will eventually fade into backward thinking in the so-called public sector as it has in the private sector. Time, nature, reason, and the human spirit will see to that. Irrespective of good intentions or the approval by consensus, nature's unrelenting feedback will gradually drive ruling political authorities to extinction.

> *Reason may be a small force, but it is constant, and works always in one direction, while the forces of unreason destroy one another in futile strife.*
> — Bertrand Russell (1872–1970)

Liberty is a self-actualized mindset of seeing and enjoying the grandeur of nature and humanity in a way that is not accessible to those adhering to politics and government. As miraculous as the universe is, it is not beyond the workings of nature, and to expect political governments to be able to defy its laws with dicta and force is to expect the unnatural.

A fundamental yet simple tenet of liberty and life is that no one owes you anything! That includes kindness, food, healthcare, education, and respect. The beauty of this tenet is that others, when left to their own devices, are inclined to respond with kindness, food, healthcare, education, and respect, without even being asked. My endless gratitude goes to all those minding their own business while caring for my every need. The belief that government can force these benefactors to take better care of me (and you) is a deep-seated, fallacious, and detrimental notion that those in the political world embrace.

For the most part, each chapter of this book comprises a stand-alone discussion.

Chapter 1, "The Political Box," discusses why so many people remain trapped in a political box, holding firmly to the illusion that politics and government serve a beneficial social function.

Chapter 2, "Barbaric Civility," discusses the duality of standards of conduct in which people condone dastardly conduct in public (political) matters that they would never think of using in their personal affairs.

Chapter 3, "Doing Good: Nice Guys Finish First," discusses the selfish nature of living organisms and the natural selection of human cooperation over force as a more adaptive behavior for surviving and propagating.

Chapter 4, "Fairness and Equality," discusses the nonsense and divisiveness of the political use of "fairness" and "equality" to disguise acts of inhumanity as moral in order to gain votes and power, while reducing the potential welfare of all.

Chapter 5, "Discrimination, Beliefs, and Expressions," discusses the importance of discrimination and how political laws prohibiting selective associations — as well as disassociations — are inhumane. The nonpolitical world is an individual one where relationships are voluntary, joint ventures based on preferences.

Chapter 6, "Tragedy of the Commons and Human Behavior," discusses how individuals achieve results that are "better than rational" when seeking ways to manage the resources of the commons, and how government intervention only obstructs the process.

Chapter 7, "Obedience to Authority," discusses the degree to which the most compassionate people can become desensitized and conduct themselves in abhorrent ways when they are obedient to authority.

Chapter 8, "Complexity, Adaption, and Order: Visualizing the Invisible Hand," discusses the multifaceted, revolutionary new science of complexity theory (also called chaos theory) that shows why the political top-down ordering of society is disruptive to social order.

Chapter 9, "Political Democracy," explores the inherent inhumanity of political democracy as a social scheme in which common sense and goodwill are scorned and individual predation upon others is praised.

Chapter 10, "A Better Life — A Better World," concludes the discussion and considers finding purpose in life while trying to make the world a better place.

1

The Political Box

The highest manifestation of life consists of this: that a being governs its own actions. A thing which is always subject to the direction of another is somewhat of a dead thing.

— Thomas Aquinas (1225–74)

A 2016 STUDY BY CHAPMAN UNIVERSITY asked 1,541 randomly selected Americans to rank their fears from a list of seventy-nine. Corrupt government officials were ranked the highest at 60 percent by the respondents, with terrorist attacks coming in second at 40 percent.[1] In a 2016 Gallup poll that asked respondents to rate the honesty and ethical standards of people from twenty-two different fields, members of Congress ranked the lowest.[2] In Canada, a 2015 poll conducted by Ipsos Reid asked people to rank their level of trust among thirty-three different professions; politicians were ranked

---

[1]Chapman University, "America's Top Fears: Chapman University Survey of American Fears," October 11, 2016, https://blogs.chapman.edu/wilkinson/2016/10/11/americas-top-fears-2016/.

[2]Gallup, "Honesty/Ethics in Professions," https://news.gallup.com/poll/1654/honesty-ethics-professions.aspx.

third from the bottom at 6 percent by respondents, with rankings ranging from 77 percent to 4 percent for all professions.[3] Moreover, a 2015 Pew Research Center study found that in every national poll conducted since 2007, fewer than three in ten Americans have expressed trust in their federal government.[4] According to the report, this decline began in 1960, when public trust was at 73 percent.

Despite this seemingly high level of fear and distrust, most people still adhere to the notion that politics and government serve a useful purpose and provide social benefits. They can't imagine a society without politics and government and, for the most part, believe all that is needed is for someone to "fix it." Dicta and force are the heart and soul of governments, and as such, they are not fixable. Even some libertarians remain trapped in the political box, convinced that the US government can be fixed and does in fact serve a useful purpose, provided its use of dicta and force is limited to areas authorized by the Constitution. Such a stance begs the question as to why some matters are better off when allowed to operate in a free market, while other matters are better off when prohibited from operating in a free market.

Those in government see solutions to problems they are certain will work. Yet they discover and rediscover that when their solutions are adopted and enforced the problems either get worse or create other problems worse than the ones for which the solution was designed. The War on Poverty (originating with President Lyndon Johnson in

---

[3]Daniel Tencer, "Canada's Most and Least Trusted Professions: Sorry, CEOx and Politicians," *HuffPost*, January 20, 2015, http://www.huffingtonpost.ca/2015/01/20/most-least-trusted-professions-canada_n_6510232.html.

[4]Pew Research Center, "Beyond Distrust: How Americans View Their Government," November 23, 2015, http://people-press.org/2015/11/23/1-trust-in-government-1958-2015/. Trend sources: Pew Research Center, National Election Studies, Gallup, ABC Washington Post, CBS New York Times, and CNN Polls.

1964) not only has failed, but has also left more poverty in its wake and ruined more families than if the government had simply done nothing.[5] In his 1984 book *Losing Ground*, Charles Murray recounts the tragic consequences that followed the adoption of governmental social policies between 1950 and 1980 and explains why such consequences are predictable wherever welfare entitlement programs are instituted. The government's "War on Drugs" (fashioned by President Richard Nixon in 1969) is an example of how using social engineering to solve one problem created another even worse by fostering more crime and havoc than if the "war" had never begun.

> Simply prohibit by law an activity you don't like and provide entitlements to those you feel need help, and we will all experience a better world! So simple, so direct, and yet so destructive!

The idea of solving problems by way of volition, where solutions evolve heuristically from the bottom up without a top-down directive, is not an easy concept to envision. In fact, there is nothing concrete to envision, since bottom-up solutions involve an evolutionary process of trial and error with the emergence of multiple, potentially viable solutions. The worthiness of any given solution is a function of the marketplace in which worthiness is determined by potential beneficiaries. In contrast, a top-down political process is a one-size-fits-all solution in which worthiness is predetermined by the designer. Chapters 6 and 8 will explore the natural bottom-up emergence of solutions to social problems and the miraculous evolutionary process in light of the fascinating new science of chaos, complexity, and spontaneous order.

It is no surprise that so many well-meaning people are trapped in the political box and never able to escape. From early childhood, we are inundated with newspapers,

---

[5]Michael Janofsky, *New York Times*, 9 February 1998.

magazines, radio, TV, and even family members filling our heads with the notion that we need someone to run our lives and take care of us. We are encouraged to participate in the political arena and debate ideas about how government should best rule us. We memorize by rote the tenets of government and pledge our allegiance to a political regime — whatever it might stand for — with little understanding of what is said or meant. Songs are sung, books are written, and movies are made that glorify wars and battles between "us" and "them," wherein heroes are honored for dutifully serving their country and dying while trying to kill people they have no actual grudge against. We are swept away by the notion of the virtuous "us" and the evil "them." The history books in our schools are filled with details of every war, where political leaders of the time gain honor and recognition with statues and monuments dedicated to them. Most American children attend state schools — the very foundation of which is political — with strict, state-approved curricula. Consequently, it's easy to see how so many become trapped for life and are unable to even consider markets, laws, justice, and societies that do not require intervention by political rulers. Ideas that challenge the utility of political intervention are mostly shrugged off with little, if any, deliberation as nonsensical or simply out of touch with reality.

Those who are not predisposed to liberty will likely find the thoughts expressed here too strange to warrant serious consideration. But equally strange is the idea that liberty is not about a consensus, since that is a political concept. Liberty is a personal affair that does not require the indulgence of others. Those inclined to liberty accept their lives as their own responsibility, take responsibility for their actions, and view those claiming to be their masters as charlatans. Being responsible for your life includes being wary of the state, just as you would be wary of any other form of intrusion. The level of state intrusion a person is willing to tolerate is an individual threshold, and the action taken when exceeded is a matter of personal judgment.

Despite the constant barrage of political indoctrination, a growing number of people have been able to escape the ideological trappings of government and engage the rational world outside the charade of politics. The booming interest in recent years in libertarian ideas and the growing disillusionment with politics and government are probably not due to any new facts, considering that history is replete with the nastiness and disasters of political intrusions into people's lives. More likely, they are due to the discovery that there are others — many others, in fact — who share similar convictions about the disutility of government. The information age of freewheeling ideas has given those holding such convictions a sense that they are not some odd, lonely fish in a large pond. This realization has led to open discussions and a deeper understanding of human nature and nature's laws, which provide a rationale for their inherent inclinations. Discussions about the disutility of government were rare some fifty years ago, but today they are common. In 1962, when I was first introduced to libertarian ideas via FEE, there were just a handful of such organizations. Today, there are hundreds of organizations teaching and preaching the virtues of liberty and the disutility of government.

The apparent rise of such candor about politics and government is partly attributable to the ugliness of the political process itself, irrespective of the social disasters it causes. Watching political debates, now available to everyone via television and the internet, is enough to disgust anyone — or at least make one wonder how such behavior can result in anything of value. The debates showcase mature men and women squabbling like spoiled children over who is better at ruling and running your life, who then have the chutzpah to ask for your blessing! Whether or not they mean well doesn't matter. Nature doesn't give a hoot about meaning or intentions; it responds to *physical* acts.

Over the past fifty years, there have been major scientific developments in genetics, evolutionary psychology, experimental game theory, economics of the commons, and complexity theory that demonstrate why we behave the way we do and how order emerges volitionally from simple, local rules. We will touch on each of these areas of study in chapters 3, 6, and 8. These exciting developments may give those who are enamored with political government the wherewithal to venture outside the quick and dirty world of political dicta and force.

Those enamored with government insist that we should be thankful for our government because it has allowed us greater freedom than other governments. When governments limit what they disallow, some feel that which is *not* disallowed is a special privilege deserving of gratitude. Allowing freedom to whatever extent government decrees requires the subjugation of some to the will of another. The issue of subjugation is not that some prefer to be subject to the will of a master, it is that those who so prefer a master require everyone else, irrespective of their preference, to be subject to the same master. As Goethe observed, "None are more hopelessly enslaved than those who falsely believe they are free."[6]

Certainly, we learn from and respect those who are wiser and can help guide us through life, but wisdom does not reside in those who *demand* respect. In the political world, those who demand respect are enforcers to be dreaded, not leaders to be followed.

---

[6]Johann Wolfgang von Goethe, *Die Wahlverwandtschaften* (English: *Elective Affinities*), bk. 2 (1809).

2

Barbaric Civility

WHILE NATURE DOES NOT HAVE a sense of good and evil or moral and immoral acts, feedback from man's conduct has led to a vocabulary that describes them. We call conduct "good" and "moral" when it leads to our well-being and "evil" and "immoral" when it leads to unhappiness. The Golden Rule[1] and certain tenets of the Ten Commandments reflect the codification of millennia of observed relationships between conduct and consequences (i.e., feedback). Most significant is natural selection, which sculpts our brains (minds) and bodies with greater fitness given changing climates, available resources, and competing life-forms.

The fitness of our brains is suited to living in small groups of fifty or so, the condition that prevailed from the time hominids emerged some six million years ago to just a

---

[1]At the British New Testament Conference in 2007, it was noted that most often in the literature of the early church, the Golden Rule appears in a negative form: "*Don't* do unto others what you would *not* have them to do unto you." The more common version today is in the positive form: "Do unto others as you would have them do unto you." The positive version can be problematic because it implies that it would be acceptable for a person to meddle in the affairs of another provided the meddler would likewise appreciate the same thing done in return.

few millennia ago. As a result, when we interact with others in small groups, our instincts tell us — without much deliberation — that we can achieve our goals with less effort and conflict when the means to achieve them align with the Golden Rule. In a family, neighborhood, business relationship, or similar small group, most of us will instinctively use the principle of the Golden Rule as our guide. In small settings, people see acts of aggression against fellow humans as uncivil, yet many of them accept such behavior as civil conduct when applied to larger social groups.

Ironically, even those who are deeply entrenched in politics act quite civilly in their own social settings of family, friends, neighbors, and associates, but abandon such conduct when dealing with those outside their personal settings. The most politically minded person would never consider extorting funds from one neighbor to aid another, but will eagerly endorse every form of extortion when the enforcer and the victim are personally unknown. The most paradoxical of such dichotomous behavior is exhibited by those of religious faiths, who celebrate the godliness of brotherly love and condemn the sinfulness of theft and killing but nevertheless endorse the political state and its inherent nature of coercion, theft, and war.

Those who conduct themselves one way in a private setting while endorsing the opposite behavior in a public (political) setting don't sense the dichotomy. In a public setting, they are mindful of the intent to solve problems and help others, but are totally *unmindful* of the uncivilized and destructive acts involved which they would clearly condemn in a private setting. The inability to sense the dichotomy between the abhorrent use of dicta and force in personal affairs and their advocacy in public affairs is unsurprising, considering the relentless political rhetoric that desensitizes our ability to discern the difference. We are awash in double-standard political jargon that manipulates our minds into transforming uncivil private behavior into civil public behavior. Moreover, we are taught to revere a constitution that authorizes those very intrusions into our lives we are told it was designed to *prevent*.

In political parlance, behavior depends on the actor, not the act. The same act that would land a private person in jail is praised when done by a so-called public one. The first actor is viewed as a criminal and the second a civil servant. Yet such an adopted double standard does not alter the negative effect on society from similar acts of conduct, irrespective of their source. Only individuals act: cities, states, and nations are incapable of doing so. Similar acts, whether by a private hoodlum or public servant, have similar social and economic consequences. Given that the use of force doesn't work in the private sector, it will not work in the public sector either, regardless of whether someone is trying to reduce poverty, improve medical care, aid the needy, or render justice.

Why do people today have a deeply held conviction that slavery is inhumane and demeans the very essence of life, yet will condone and even enthusiastically endorse enslavement when the state is the master? To condemn a plantation owner for reaping the fruit of another man's labor against his will, while commending the state for doing the same is an obvious contradictory stance, unless one considers slavery to be humane if given the "right master." Slavery in any form is demeaning to life, and those who subordinate themselves to a ruling master — whether that master is a king, statesman, or plantation owner — demean their own lives in particular. This does not suggest that one should simply ignore the demands of a master or ruler, since the consequences of disobedience are often worse than those of obedience. However, obedience to a master or ruler does not imply that it is their *due*.

In time, the idea of a righteous political master will become an anachronism, as has a righteous slave master — not because of any concerted effort, but simply due to the futility of trying to suppress the human spirit with threats of punishment. As strange as it may be for people today to envision civil life *outside* the political box, their distant descendants will likely find the same strangeness in the idea of civil life *within* it.

Our inherent moral compass guides us toward volitional cooperation as a superior, self-serving means to enhance our personal well-being and, subsequently, social well-being. We instinctively sense the use of force as a risky and less rewarding means to well-being. This natural inclination toward cooperation and away from force tends to bring out the best behavior in people. In direct contrast, government authorities insist that dicta, obedience, and punishment are necessary to bring out the best behavior in people who, if left to their own volition, would become savages in a lawless society. There is abundant literature to dispel this notion which we will touch upon in chapters 6 and 8.

By demanding that every child attend school and by making so-called free public schools available, government authorities create a perpetual forum to indoctrinate the young as they proceed through their chambers, convinced that good citizenship means respect for political officials and obedience to their demands. Without this subtle mental conditioning, governments would be unable to maintain obedience to their dicta since brute force alone is too obvious, inefficient, and costly.

For the most part, all that is required to assess the beauty and wonderment of liberty and recognize the disutility of political dicta and force is common sense — a gift we inherited from our ancestors. We are not born with an empty slate, as John Locke suggested, but begin life with myriad built-in instincts and common sense that evolved through natural selection. Selfishness is the nature of life, and it drives us to acquire resources and secure mating opportunities in ways we perceive to be the most optimal. Nature's culling by way of feedback slowly worked its way to favor our ancestors using cooperation in lieu of force as a more adaptive behavior for survival and propagation. That process continues, and recognizing it can help us see through the charade and disutility of political governments with their doctrine of punishment for disobedience to their dicta.

3

Doing Good:
Nice Guys Finish First

THE NOTION THAT ANIMAL BEHAVIOR evolved for the good of
the species was a longstanding myth that met its demise
as a result of the work of several biologists. In the mid-
1960s, George Williams[1] and William Hamilton[2] first proposed the idea that animal behavior evolved for the good
of the gene, which Richard Dawkins later called "the selfish gene." When Dawkins came to this conclusion, he was
stunned: "We are survival machines — robot vehicles
blindly programmed to preserve the selfish molecules
known as genes." He added: "This is a truth that fills me
with astonishment. Though I have known it for years, I
never get fully used to it."[3]

Today, literature abounds in support of their findings,
showing indeed that all animals — including humans —
act individually to replicate their genes. However, the idea

---

[1]George C. Williams, *Adaptation and Natural Selection: A Critique of Some Current Evolutionary Thought* (Princeton, NJ: Princeton University Press, 1996).

[2]W. J. Hamilton, "The Genetical Evolution of Social Behaviour," *Journal of Theoretical Biology* 2 (1964): 17–52.

[3]Richard Dawkins, *The Selfish Gene* (Oxford: Oxford University Press, 1976).

of genetic individualism did not comport with the agendas of certain political groups; as a result, several university lectures in support of these findings were disrupted by student protesters.

As a target of such disruption, Edward O. Wilson notes:

> But as we shall see as the new IQ wars develop over the coming months [they have since proved virulent on the anti-genetic side], as ideologues on both sides spring into their accustomed positions, feeling good is not what science is all about. Getting it right, and then basing social decisions on tested and carefully weighed objective knowledge, is what science is all about.[4]

Disruptive tactics of this sort are common in the political world, where prohibition replaces reason and persuasion. Nevertheless, the study of sociobiology, which expanded into evolutionary biology and evolutionary psychology, continues to gain acceptance, with ever more studies showing why we — along with other animals — act the way we do, based on the metaphorical "selfish gene" model.

Helping others based on their degrees of relatedness is a well-established behavior observed in all animals, where, for example, an individual's genes are, on average, equivalent to the genes carried by two siblings or eight cousins. As such, helping kin makes good evolutionary sense based on that model since the actors are more or less helping themselves (i.e., their own genes).

It also makes evolutionary sense to help those from whom we receive or expect reciprocity. Cooperation evolved in many animals when sharing food became essential, whenever a find was rare or sporadic, or when

---

[4] Edward O. Wilson, "Science and Ideology," *Academic Questions* 8 (1995), http://hiram-caton.com/documents/Evolution/Science%20and%20ideology.pdf.

a group effort improved the chances of catching prey. Of course, one of the most ubiquitous cooperative ways to copy genes is mating.

Humans are by far the most cooperative of all animals. Social exchange is a human universal that is expressed in all cultures.[5] Elaborate social networks have evolved wherein individuals cooperate in the exchange of goods and services with trading counterparts they do not even know.[6] Selfishness is the bilateral driving force behind markets, where people satisfy their own selfish preferences by satisfying the selfish, but different, preferences of others. Mating and markets have the same fundamentals: "I have *this* to make you happy, and you have *that* to make me happy."

One's reputational trademark is the catalyst that nurtures cooperative behavior. A reputation can expedite new relationships when *good* and impede them when *bad*, giving each of us a powerful incentive to acquire one and avoid the other. Furthermore, the sensitivity of an ongoing assessment of our behavior warns us that, while a good reputation takes time to build, it can disappear in an instant following a single breach.

To build trust and cooperation in the marketplace with traders who are unrelated to us requires an effective "cheater detection" trait.[7] As H. Clark Barrett explains: "Evolutionary analyses have shown that social exchange cannot evolve unless individuals are able to detect those who cheat. Therefore, from an evolutionary standpoint, the function of detecting acts of cheating is to connect them

---

[5]Wikipedia, s.v., "Cultural universal," https://en.wikipedia.org/wiki/Cultural_universal.

[6]I refer to cooperation here and elsewhere as a voluntary act but do acknowledge that it can also occur if the participant is forced or threatened to cooperate when the perceived cost of being cooperative (obedient) is less than that of being uncooperative (disobedient).

[7]Leda Cosmides, H. Clark Barrett, and John Tooby, "Adaptive Specializations, Social Exchange, and the Evolution of Human Intelligence," *PNAS* 107, Suppl. 2 (2010): 9007–9014.

to an identity — to deduce character."[8] Robert Trivers, William Hamilton, Robert Axelrod, and other evolutionary researchers use game theory to understand the conditions under which social exchange can and cannot evolve. For adaptations causing this form of cooperation to evolve and persist (i.e., to embody what evolutionary game theorists call an *evolutionarily stable strategy* [ESS]), cooperators must have mechanisms that perform specific tasks. For example, reciprocation cannot evolve if the organism lacks reasoning procedures that can effectively detect cheaters (i.e., those who take conditionally offered benefits without providing the promised return). Such individuals would be open to exploitation and selected out.[9]

We are fairly good at picking up on someone's character; even their most insignificant mannerisms can signal "I can trust this person" or "I can't trust this person." Such a knack for detection also selects for cheaters capable of putting up a better deceptive front.

Noted evolutionary psychologists Leda Cosmides and John Tooby hypothesize that the human neurocognitive architecture includes *social contract algorithms*: a set of programs (neural circuits) that natural selection specialized for solving the intricate computational problems inherent in adaptively engaging in social-exchange behavior, including a subroutine for cheater detection.[10]

Because cheaters (free riders) gain a benefit without a cost, they depend on the resourcefulness of those who do bear the cost.[11] In the upside-down political world,

---

[8]Andrea Estrada, "Brain Mechanism Evolved to Identify Those With a Propensity to Cheat, According to UCSB Scientists," May 11, 2010, http://www.ia.ucsb.edu/pa/display.aspx?pkey=2243.

[9]Center for Evolutionary Psychology, New Page 1, https://www.cep.ucsb.edu/socex/sugiyama.html.

[10]Ibid.

[11]Getting a benefit without bearing a cost is not cheating if that benefit is an externality, such as that deriving from a neighbor's streetlight or his beautiful yard, which someone other than the owner can enjoy without

individuals are not only incentivized to cheat, they are defended against those who detect them as cheaters and who would otherwise ostracize them. In that world, cheaters gain entitlement to that which they did *not* work to produce, while those who would ostracize them as cheaters are disentitled to that which they *have* worked to produce. It is natural to ostracize able-bodied slackers who do not pull their weight in hunts, the workplace, or wherever joint work is customary, yet still expect to share in the goods that are produced. Even those with a strong political bent have a sense of repugnancy toward able-bodied slackers encountered in their personal affairs but will, however, endorse entitlement programs that encourage slacking in the public arena.

Although there is a clear adaptive value in helping those who are genetically related or who reciprocate benefits in a cooperative exchange, why would there be adaptive value for what appears to be altruistic behavior (bearing a cost without gaining an offsetting benefit) where kinship and reciprocity are lacking? Not only are humans the most cooperative beings, they may be alone or in rare company when it comes to helping those where kinship and reciprocity are absent. In humans, there is a natural moral sentiment that engenders empathy and drives us to want to do good for others. We sense both the pain and the pleasure that others feel. Caring about others may seem to conflict with our innate selfish nature, but deeper within us is the long-range, personal benefit we gain from it.

The Theory of Moral Sentiments, written by Adam Smith in 1759, begins with the following assertion:

> How selfish soever man may be supposed, there are evidently some principles in his nature, which interest him in the fortune of others, and render their happiness necessary to him, though he derives nothing

---

diminishing its benefits or increasing its cost for the owner.

from it, except the pleasure of seeing it. Of this kind is pity or compassion, the emotion which we feel for the misery of others, when we either see it, or are made to conceive it in a very lively manner. That we often derive sorrow from the sorrows of others, is a matter of fact too obvious to require any instances to prove it; for this sentiment, like all the other original passions of human nature, is by no means confined to the virtuous and humane, though they perhaps may feel it with the most exquisite sensibility. The greatest ruffian, the most hardened violator of the laws of society, is not altogether without it.[12]

In *An Inquiry into the Nature and Causes of the Wealth of Nations*, published in 1776, Smith asserts:

It is not from the benevolence of the butcher, the brewer, or the baker that we expect our dinner, but from their regard to their own interest. We address ourselves not to their humanity but to their self-love, and never talk to them of our own necessities, but of their advantages.[13]

These two seemingly divergent assertions are quite compatible in light of twentieth-century studies in evolutionary psychology.

When we donate to charitable causes, help strangers, adopt abandoned children, assist the unfortunate, defend the defenseless, comfort the ill, or even care for an injured bird, we experience a sense of euphoria — that warm, feel-good sensation that drives us to such behavior. Paul Zak and others claim that oxytocin gives us that feel-good sensation we

---

[12]Adam Smith, *The Theory of Moral Sentiments* (Digireads.com 2010), 1.

[13]Adam Smith, *An Inquiry into the Nature and Causes of the Wealth of Nations*, 6th ed. (New York: Modern Library, 1994), p. 15.

experience when we connect with the feelings of others. In game theory sessions, participants who received a nasal infusion of oxytocin showed improved cooperation and increased generosity. Generosity may be part of the human repertoire to sustain cooperative relationships. Oxytocin has also been shown to increase the ability to intuit people's intentions from their facial expressions.[14] In a 2012 article, Songfa Zhong and coauthors state:

> It is difficult to overstate the role of trust in facilitating the smooth functioning of social and market institutions in modern societies. Trust can provide the basis for reducing social complexity, enhancing social order and social capital, as well as overcoming the inherent risk involved in economic exchange and social interaction.[15]

This do-good, feel-good scenario must have adaptive value for it to exist in almost everyone, irrespective of their culture. It likely served our ancestors, as it does us, as an effective signaling mechanism to inform others that we are trustworthy and cooperative members of the group. Although these sentiments are genuine, they nevertheless remain self-serving, with the resulting adaptive advantages of increased resource acquisition and mating opportunities. Yes, in the long run, nice guys *do* finish first!

However, people can deceptively display that same signaling behavior to gain acceptance when actual empathy is lacking and trust is unjustified. Politicians are adept at manipulating their way to power by stroking people's heartstrings, pretending to be charitable when, in fact,

---

[14]Paul J. Zak, Angela A. Stanton, and Sheila Ahmadi, "Oxytocin Increases Generosity in Humans," *Nature* 435 (2005): 673–76.

[15]Songfa Zhong, Mikhail Monakhov, Helen P. Mok, Terry Tong, Poh San Lai, Soo Hong Chew, Richard P. Ebstin, "U-Shaped Relation between Plasma Oxytocin Levels and Behavior in the Trust Game," *PLoS One* 7, 12 (2012): e51095.

they are only offering to share that which the state has plundered from others. Such gestures are *not* charitable, because charity implies a cost to the donor. Politicians who use such deception to win the votes of recipients of this "generosity" can also gain support from those who ride their coattails as an indirect way of signaling their own charitable nature. Being charitable and considerate of others are good-natured acts, but *only* when the actor is being charitable and considerate with that which is *his or hers*.

There are few who are not touched when they learn about the gracious behavior of one person toward another when they sense it to be a sincere act of moral sentiment. Books and movies captivate us with such scenes that trigger those tear-jerking neurotransmitters that make us feel good and eager to come back for more. Helping the helpless triggers a warm sensation in all of us, but when we are *forced* to help, those sensations are not only lost, they are replaced with feelings of resentment and anger toward those who plunder us while claiming charitable credit and, to some degree, toward those who receive the help, especially when those persons are not truly helpless.

To further their deceptive signaling of compassion to garner votes, politicians are adept at riling up their supporters by making them the victims of a targeted culprit. This divisive tactic of pitting one group against another in a culprit-victim scenario is further evidence of how government brings out the worst in people. Targeting the rich as the "greedy culprit" of the "victimized poor," men as the "ungracious culprit" of "victimized women," and whites as the "oppressive culprit" of "victimized blacks" has become a common political practice. In fact, pitting neighbor against neighbor is so common in a political democracy that we find ourselves desensitized to the brutality of such conduct in which people are tricked and sacrificed for the sake of someone's desire to gain political power and prestige.

In *The Road to Serfdom*, F. A. Hayek states: "The contrast between the 'we' and the 'they' is consequently always employed by those who seek the allegiance of the masses."[16] These divisive tactics drive people to take sides, foster adversarial political parties, and launch campaigns to commandeer the masses to join the fray.

Caring about others is not synonymous with helping them. Within a society, those seeking to benefit themselves, who produce and provide goods and services others find beneficial, offer the greatest help to others. These benefactors may not even know or care about those they are helping. All they know is that by benefiting some people with their goods and services, they will in turn become beneficiaries of the goods and services other people provide.

A desire for people to live longer is not a requirement for discovering better medicines any more than producing food requires a desire to prevent famine. Scientists discover medicines because people prefer wellness to illness, and farmers produce food because people prefer full bellies to empty ones, thus giving each of them the opportunity to prosper by satisfying those preferences.

When we hear via the political network that the wealthy should sacrifice and give back to society, common sense is all we need to tell us that such talk is nothing but political balderdash. Sacrifice is genetically nonsensical because our "selfish" genes are not inclined to allow such destructive behavior. Our unrelenting genetic selfishness produces all the goods and services that bring about a prosperous society. The volitional transfer of goods and services is a mutually self-serving act in which each party takes advantage of the other — with a mutual invitation to be taken advantage of. Since a mutual exchange of advantages is voluntary, neither party has anything to give back. Only those who take advantage of others absent their volition owe anything back.

---

[16]F. A. Hayek, *The Road to Serfdom* (University of Chicago Press, 1944), p. 139.

So-called charitable help is negligible in comparison to routine, 24/7 commercial help. Moreover, charity as an entitlement has the inherent risk of destructive dependency that precludes personal achievement and gaining meaning to one's life.

Thomas Sowell argues:

> You cannot take any people, of any color, and exempt them from the requirements of civilization — including work, behavioral standards, personal responsibility and all the other basic things that the clever intelligentsia disdain — without ruinous consequence to them and society at large. Nonjudgmental subsidies of counterproductive lifestyles are treating people as if they were livestock, to be fed and tended by others in a welfare state and yet expecting them to develop as human beings.[17]

Those entrenched within the political box are often unable to distinguish between that which is called help and that which is truly helpful to others. Political programs in the name of welfare are human tragedies that display the act of caring but ignore the damaging effect upon the very people the endorsers claim to be helping. One of the most inhumane concepts promulgated by those of the political world is that by making goods and services "free" we can improve human welfare. When "welfare" and "entitlement" programs are shown to be destructive and inhumane, the standard political retort is to disparage the messenger, accusing him of being uncaring, cold-hearted, and greedy.

Some may find personal gratification in taking from some to give to others, but such predatory conduct cannot

---

[17]Thomas Sowell, "Race, Politics and Lies," RealClearPolitics.com, May 5, 2015, https://www.realclearpolitics.com/articles/2015/05/05/race_politics_and_lies_126484.html.

be admired as humanitarian, given that it reduces social welfare by diminishing productivity, engendering discord, and demeaning the lives of recipients. Furthermore, the predatory conduct by some will cause others to do the same, since no one wants to be taken for a sucker.

Myriad government welfare programs have been devised, each with a common thread of predation as the means to improve human welfare. Yet, despite the negative consequences of such programs, politicians remain convinced that predation — taking from some to give to others — if done their way, can avoid the negative results of prior attempts and, instead, actually improve social welfare. The negative social results from such predatory policies can easily be predicted with only a rudimentary understanding of human nature. The Pilgrims of Plymouth learned about human nature firsthand by observing their own behavior when governed by two dramatically different policies that were employed during separate time periods. The distinct contrast of their behavior during the run of one period to that of the other is extensively documented in the diary of Governor William Bradford which will be discussed in chapter 6, The Tragedy of the Commons and Human Behavior.

People may claim nature to be too harsh — arguing that good intentions should be rewarded, or that the feedback is more favorable to some but less to others and thus unfair — but nature's laws are unyielding to human hope, wishes, and beliefs. Simply believing in the unnatural is not harmful, but when those holding such beliefs gain political power and use humans as laboratory animals to impose their beliefs, their acts are inhumane, irrespective of their intent.

Such is the theater of politics, a dreadful scene in which humanity is up for public sacrifice.

4

Fairness and Equality

There is, in fact, a manly and lawful passion
for equality which excites men to wish all to be
powerful and honored. This passion tends to
elevate the humble to the rank of the great; but
there exists also in the human heart a depraved
taste for equality, which impels the weak to
attempt to lower the powerful to their own level,
and reduces men to prefer equality in slavery to
inequality with freedom.

— Alexis de Tocqueville (1805–59)

IN THE POLITICAL WORLD, ONE way to get what isn't yours is
to stage a public demonstration claiming unfairness and
inequity. Outside the political world, when people want
what others have, they either trade for it with labor or
goods or take it by force. The latter is a risky and generally costly choice. However, in the political world, you can
acquire what isn't yours by petitioning the state to take it
for you without facing the hazards of taking it yourself.

Few weeks pass without a riot or demonstration break-
ing out with protesters demanding from the state just
about everything: food, shelter, health care, higher pay,

lower prices, equality, *ad infinitum*. It's difficult to blame the protesters since the state, after all, holds itself out as the great provider of whatever the populace wants in exchange for votes and support. Protesters should not be expected to analyze or even care about the true source of these provisions. Like the rest of us, they are simply acting in their own self-interest. Certainly, they are acquiring resources taken from others against their will, but the idea that such takings by the state is theft, immoral, or unjust is too esoteric for most to even give them pause. Political propaganda has instilled into many of us that, in the interest of "fairness," the less wealthy are entitled to some of what belongs to the wealthier. Absent political motivation there is no valid basis for such a notion.

An effective ploy for mustering supporters to a political camp is to provoke their anger with notions of unfairness and inequality. "Join my camp," a politician might say, "and together we can get our fair share of the wealth the rich are unfairly keeping from us." Year after year, the political offerings grow, enticing an ever-larger portion of the populace into the parasitic fold. When the political diatribe of pitting the poor against the rich has successfully corralled the votes of the poorest, politicians then ratchet up the campaign, pitting middle-income earners against the rich in a bid to lure even more voters. Finally, when that campaign has run its course, political attention expands to lure nearly every other voter into the political camp by pitting them against the richest 1 percent. In recent years, the banners and posters of protesters proclaiming themselves to be the victimized "99 percenters" exemplify the success of such campaigning.

Such deceitful behavior by politicians in their quest for power should be too obvious and repugnant to gain the support of anyone with any sense of decency and the ability to reason. However, that is not the case: even the most mindful person can be conditioned by the constant flow of propaganda to condone such political rhetoric and chicanery.

Outside the political world, fairness is not a matter of comparative personal achievement but rather a complimentary description of character. Fairness describes a person who plays by the rules and is courteous and honest. Fairness and unfairness reflect how well or poorly people treat others, *not* how they compare with or differ from them. Being rich or poor is neither fair nor unfair: it is simply a measurement of a person's monetary wealth compared to that of others. However, politicians use the word "fairness" to shroud the act of theft in an aura of righteousness.

Although fairness is not a term of comparative value, for the sake of discussion, let's briefly consider it to be so and see that even in its misuse, most people would likely prefer their own life to any of the possible lives they might have lived.

First, living matter emerged in its simplest form some three to four billion years ago and then evolved into a biomass of ever more complex organisms, of which there are now some eight million known animal species, with humans ostensibly occupying the most complex position — at least when measured by cognition. The diversity of life-forms is a natural process, with natural selection fashioning each organism to better fit its own particular niche. Those who contend that inequality is unfair ignore all the lives those organisms are living that few humans would choose to live in exchange.

Second, asserting unfairness in the disparity between those of lesser and greater wealth totally ignores the preponderance of lives people once lived at a level that would make the poorest people of today far richer than the richest person of those times. We are extremely fortunate to be living now, rather than when our distant ancestors had life spans of merely thirty to forty years, scraping together just enough each day to make it to the next. Even the so-called "good old days" of our recent ancestors were quite miserable compared to the living standards of the poorest today.

Finally, and most important, politically reported inequality is only a measurement of monetary wealth, but for most people wealth encompasses far more than that. It includes love, family, friends, accomplishments, and gaining inner meaning to one's life, which trump all that the richest billionaires can buy.

People in virtually all corners of the political box take for granted that a large disparity in earnings and wealth is a problem. Even those who counter such claims only argue that the purported disparity is exaggerated because the data are either incorrect or misapplied. Some argue that using income levels to measure inequality is misleading and that consumption levels would be more appropriate. In other words, no matter how it is measured, there is an assumed political notion that a large gap in earnings, wealth, or consumption is in fact a problem.

It is a fact that some people earn more and are financially much wealthier than others, but it is *not* a fact that this disparity is a problem. To peddle the idea that it is a problem, politicos employ the *assumptive close* technique to connote, by assumption, a problem, thus bypassing the need to provide supportive evidence. People simply assume the problem exists, leaving only a method of measurement and the means to resolve it open for discussion. This shrewd sales technique is evident in the titles of articles and essays that connote the problem as a given. Here are a few examples:[1]

---

[1] Emphasis added. Christopher S. Rugaber, "Wealth Gap: A Guide to What It Is and Why It Matters," Associated Press, January 27, 2014, http://www.businessinsider.com/wealth-gap-a-guide-to-what-it-is-and-why-it-matters-2014-1; Lisa Fu, "The Wealth Gap in the U.S. Is Worse Than in Russia or Iran," August 1 2017, http://fortune.com/2017/08/01wealth-gap-america/; Heather Long, "U.S. Inequality Keeps Getting Uglier," December 22,2016, http://money.cnn.com/2016/12/22/news/economy/us-inequality-worse/index.html.

- "Inequality in America Is *Getting Worse*."

- "So, What Do Experts Say Is the *Best Way to Shrink* the Wealth Gap?"

- "Is Everyone *Concerned* About the Wealth Gap?"

- "Has the Administration Made Progress in *Narrowing* the Wealth Gap?"

- "So, Why Has Income Inequality *Worsened*?"

- "When Did this Wealth Gap *Problem* Start?"

- "*How Bad* Is the Wealth Inequality We're Seeing in the United States?"

According to Alan B. Krueger, former chairman of the White House Council of Economic Advisors, income inequality can have a variety of negative economic effects,[2] such as:

1. More income shifts to the wealthy, who tend to spend less of each marginal dollar, causing consumption — and therefore, economic growth — to slow.

2. Income mobility falls, meaning parents' income is more likely to predict their children's income.

3. Middle- and lower-income families borrow more money to maintain their consumption, which is a contributing factor to financial crises (based on the work of Raghuram Rajan and Robert Reich).

4. The wealthy gain more political power, which results in policies that further slow economic growth.

---

[2]Alan B. Krueger, "The Rise and Consequences of Inequality in the United States," speech January 12, 2012, https://cdn.americanprogress.org/wp-content/uploads/events/2012/01/pdf/krueger.pdf.

Let's examine each of Krueger's claims:

1. Income doesn't "shift" to the wealthy as if removed from one group and transferred to another. An *earner* does not make others poorer, because he or she can only be enriched by enriching someone else. As such, there isn't a shift in wealth between people but rather an increase in the wealth of each participant in a market transaction. This is the fundamental nature of markets, in which trading improves the well-being of each trader from their pre-transaction wealth level. Krueger's use of the word "shift" rejects an elemental economic principle that the economy is not a fixed pie. He then depicts greedy, rich scoundrels taking an undeserved portion of an illusionary fixed pie, thus paving a path to justify taking a larger share of their wealth through higher taxes. Disregarding the political trickery, the claim that the wealthy spend less of each marginal dollar and cause economic growth to slow is without foundation: whatever portion of earnings people do not spend, someone else will spend by accessing that money via a bank loan, whereby the borrower becomes the spending proxy of the depositor. Money doesn't simply lie dormant in a vault; the banker offsets the interest paid to depositors by earning interest from borrowers, who in turn use that money to buy houses, cars, equipment, and so on.

2. The evidence directly contradicts Krueger's claim that income mobility has fallen. In the United States, the odds of moving up or down the relative-income ladder have not changed appreciably in the last twenty years, according to an extensive 2014 study that tracked forty million children and their parents between 1996

and 2012.[3] The findings contradict claims by politicians in both major parties. As the authors of the study note, their results show broadly similar and steady mobility when compared with a previous study of children born from 1952 to 1975.[4] Taken together, these studies suggest that the rates of intergenerational mobility have held fairly steady over the last half-century, according to Raj Chetty. Relative mobility is the change in ranking of a person's household earnings compared with the earnings of others, while absolute mobility is the change in a person's actual household earnings compared with their earnings in an earlier period. Over the thirty-three–year period from 1979 to 2011, average inflation-adjusted, after-tax income — which equals market income plus government transfers minus federal taxes — grew significantly for all income quintiles. Households in the bottom quintile averaged a growth in earnings of 1.2 percent per year, thereby producing a cumulative growth of 48 percent over the thirty-three–year period. Households in the middle three quintiles (21st to 80th percentiles) had a cumulative growth of 40 percent over the same period. Consequently, most adults today have much more disposable income than their parents did at the same age.[5]

---

[3]Raj Chetty, Nathaniel Hendren, Patrick Kline, and Emmanuel Saez, "Where Is the Land of Opportunity? The Geography of Intergenerational Mobility in the United States," *Quarterly Journal of Economics* 129, no. 4 (2014).

[4]Chul-In Lee and Gary Solon, 2006, "Trends in Intergenerational Income Mobility," NBER Working Paper No. 12007, National Bureau of Economic Research, February.

[5]"The Distribution of Household Income and Federal Taxes," *Congressional Budget Office* (November 2014), p. 24.

3. Krueger's third point, that inequality means the poor and middle classes must borrow more to maintain their consumption, is a non sequitur. Although the poor and middle classes earn less than those in the higher quintiles, they are not necessarily earning less in real terms than they earned in earlier periods. Thus, maintaining consumption does not depend on comparative earnings but rather on actual earnings, which have increased substantially over time, as noted above. In other words, even if relative mobility were zero or even negative, absolute mobility determines an individual's actual change in potential consumption.

4. In criticizing the wealthy for allegedly using political power to adopt policies that slow down the economy, Krueger erroneously assumes that policies designed to accelerate the economy are good. But in fact, any policy that attempts to engineer the rate of economic growth is a disruptive and harmful intrusion.

According to Nobel Laureate Robert Shiller, "The most important problem that we are facing now today, I think, is rising inequality in the United States and elsewhere in the world."[6] He supports establishing a contingency plan now to raise taxes on the rich if inequality increases. Thomas Piketty closes his popular book *Capital in the Twenty-First Century* by recommending that governments step in now by adopting a global tax on wealth to prevent soaring inequality from contributing to economic or political instability down the road.[7] Imagine a candid politician taking

---

[6]John Christoffersen, "Nobel-winning Economist Warns: Rising Inequality a Problem." Associated Press, October 15, 2013, http://www.telegram.com/article/20131015/NEWS/310149727/1237.

[7]Thomas Piketty, *Capital in the Twenty-First Century*, reprint ed. (Cambridge, MA: Belknap Press 2017).

Shiller's and Piketty's proposals to heart: "If you find your earnings disturbing because others are earning more than you, then vote for me. I promise to get you your fair share of the wealth by embezzling it from those who earn more; this way, you avoid the hazards of embezzling it yourself or having to contend with earning more on your own."

Let's use a dramatic thought experiment to demonstrate the negative impact on the poor if the government were to forcibly reduce the earning gap. Consider whether the living standard of the poor would improve, *ipso facto*, if all the highest earners met their immediate demise. Eliminating the highest earners would surely "improve" (shrink) the earning gap. Now, the prior middle-income earners would become the country's highest earners and thus, to further "improve" the gap, they would then need to meet their demise as well. You get the picture. By continuously eliminating the wealthiest, there would eventually be perfect equality with no income gap because the poorest person would also be the richest person of the land — and have to be self-sufficient and poorer than he or she ever was before.

Alternatively, consider the following simpler and more realistic thought experiment to illustrate the obvious nonsense of a harmful wealth gap. Let's begin with a society of, say, one million people of equal earnings and wealth. While working in his shop, an ambitious young man named Tom gets the "bright" idea of a light source that is neither a candle nor a kerosene lamp. He works on his idea for a few years before ultimately designing a device that economically converts electricity into light. It's cheaper, brighter, and safer than any known light source other than the sun. It's a rather simple device that just about anybody else could have made, but Tom produces it first and calls it a light bulb. He likely wasn't interested in saving houses from burning down or brightening long winter evenings; he may have been a so-called greedy, self-serving guy, knowing only that people prefer lightness to darkness and home preservation to destruction.

Making the first light bulb may have cost several thousand dollars, but making a million may cost little more than ten cents each. One by one, people line up to buy Tom's new-fangled light bulb at twenty cents each, and he sells ten million of them. Irrespective of the financial preciseness of the transactions, each buyer improves his lifestyle immensely by an amount multiple times the meager cost of a few bulbs to light up his house. Not even through the most tortuous reasoning could one conclude that those who made Tom a millionaire also made him a scoundrel, or that their individual higher standard of living created a problem by not reaching the height of Tom's. In total, of course, the collective gain in the standard of living by the million people makes the amount Tom earned a relative pittance.

Today, innovators on the front wave of new technologies are bringing unimaginable benefits to nearly everyone in the world who volitionally launch these esteemed benefactors into stardom and wealth. These spectacular individuals are the praised "one percenters" that political pundits tell us we should despise. Such discrediting of society's greatest benefactors demonstrates how political motivation can turn otherwise honorable people into deceptive town criers.

Anyone truly concerned about the gap between their own earnings and those of a higher earner can always decline to buy the goods and services the latter offers, thus helping to "even things out." However, those with lower earnings aren't foolish; they know their purchases will make others richer, yet eagerly continue to buy their goods and services, which makes better sense than trying to produce these same items themselves. Self-sufficiency is always available to take a stand against making others richer, but few ever choose that route.

People's wealth reflects society's appreciation of the value of their work — assuming, of course, that they justly earned it. However, wealth gained by force, deceit, or obtaining privileges from the government, such as subsidies or restrictions imposed on competition, is not an accurate reflection of society's appreciation and valuation.

The implication that high inequality of earnings is a moral crime is tantamount to praising a bank robber who is trying to reduce inequality between himself and the bank owner and, as such, doing his best to reduce crime. One would have to be most gullible to fall prey to the devious political tactic of criminalizing wealth, victimizing poorness, and moralizing theft.

There are many reasons why some earn more than others. For instance, some people are taller than others and, statistically, the taller you are, the more you earn — by a purported annual average of $789 per inch.[8] Attractive employees earn, on average, roughly 5 percent more than unattractive employees, according to a study by Daniel Hamermesh.[9] It would be just as foolish to claim that this disparity in height and beauty is a crime. It is simply a fact that some people are taller, richer, better looking, and smarter than others, but it does not follow that everyone would be better off if no one were taller, richer, better looking, or smarter than anyone else.

Those who live more sensible lives outside the political box are undaunted by the political rhetoric of unfairness and inequality. Instead, they simply strive to improve their own quality of life without fretting over someone across town, across the country, or even overseas being taller, richer, better looking, or smarter, or, in effect, experiencing a better quality of life than their own.

In *A Theory of Justice*, noted political philosopher John Rawls (1921–2002) claims that justice must deny a person the financial benefits resulting from his or her natural talent, since such talents were "accidents of natural

---

[8]Timothy A. Judge and Daniel M. Cable, "The Effect of Physical Height on Workplace Success and Income: Preliminary Test of a Theoretical Mode," *Journal of Applied Psychology* 89, no. 3 (2004): 428–41.

[9]Daniel Hamermesh and Jeff E. Biddle, "Beauty and the Labor Market," *American Economic Review* (1994): 1174–94.

endowment" and not earned.[10] Such an intrusive notion begs the question: Why would it then follow that some-one's "unearned" financial benefit has been earned by or belongs to anyone else? Underlying such intrusive-ness is an almost divine-like arrogance asserting that all lives must be lived in accordance with another's personal agenda. Only in a political democracy would anyone dare assert such a pretentious concept without being laughed out of the room as an eccentric demigod.

To demonstrate the arrogance and intrusiveness of Rawls's claim, let's ask Rawls to personally carry out on one of his wealthier neighbors his claim of fairness and justice. Imagine the scene: Rawls is knocking on his neigh-bor's door. When answered, he demands as a matter of fairness and justice that the neighbor share his house with others because the neighbor was able to acquire it only as a result of his greater talent. Rather than calling the police, the neighbor would likely call one of Rawls's family mem-bers to tend to Rawls's safety, fearing that the poor fellow had totally lost his sense of reason. The absurdity of advo-cating these types of political "fairness" claims in the name of justice can easily be seen for what they are — whether logically, emotionally, economically, or morally — by reducing them to similar scenes involving just two actors. For some, reducing a scene to a one-on-one interaction to distill and analyze the essence of a political claim is quite natural; but for others — particularly those trapped in the typical political box — such an exercise is generally too abstruse.

Aside from the arrogant and intrusive nature of Rawls's claim that people do not deserve the financial benefit of their natural talents, the glaring fallacy of that claim resides in the fact that the more talented people are at satisfying the preferences of others, the wealthier they become — but to no greater extent than the sum value of the benefits (wealth,

---

[10]John Rawls, *A Theory of Justice* (Cambridge, MA: Belknap Press 1971).

pleasure, health, etc.) realized by those whose preferences they have satisfied. The choices people make determine the value of another's talent. To handicap naturally talented people in their pursuit of well-being is to simultaneously handicap those who would choose to benefit from that talent in their own pursuit of well-being. Satirically, in a Rawlsian world, talented people would be restrained from overburdening society with the benefits of their talent.

Beneath the fallacy that earning gaps are harmful and wealthy people cause others to have less is the *demoralizing creation of anger* in people who now live their lives blaming others for their lot in life. This sorrowful outcome is just another example of how government brings out the worst in people — in this case, both in those who create the anger and those who now harbor it.

5

Discrimination, Beliefs, and Expressions

The more prohibitions you have, the less virtuous people will be.

— Lao Tzu (604–531 BC)

WHEN WE DISCRIMINATE, WE MAKE a distinction either in favor of or against a person, thing, or idea based on our personal inclinations. Our preferences can't ignore our inner prejudices and biases. The ideas expressed in this book will no doubt trigger some of those deeper biases that will lead one to either condemn or endorse them. Life is a mental process of building and rebuilding a foundational philosophy, serving as a guide to gauge and judge our acceptance or rejection of ideas expressed by others. When we hear a political statement, we not only instantly accept or reject it, but often form an instant favorable or unfavorable impression of the speaker as well.

We feel more comfortable with people of a similar culture who speak our language and share our customs than we do with those very different from ourselves. Infants find a face of a different color or unfamiliar features unnatural and alarming, as shown by their increased heart rates.[1] The strangeness of people of different cultures or with different features generally fades when they become personally known.

Regardless of the source, it would be naïve to expect certain discriminatory feelings to disappear by prohibiting their expression. Besides, ignoring biases and prejudices in the context of long-term personal relationships would be irrational. Marriage, for example, involves critical gender, age, race, and religious discriminations. We don't simply propose marriage indiscriminately to the next person we encounter; we choose a mate based on that inner sense that triggers a yea or a nay, even when we don't necessarily know why or whether the choice is rational.

Nearly everyone would consider it foolish to propose an intimate relationship such as marriage to someone of a race, ethnicity, religion, gender, or age that is not to their liking or preference — or worse, that they despise. Yet, in the workplace, that same selective rationale, if detected or suspected, is punishable by law. When we propose marriage or a job position, we express a preference to associate with that person in a given relationship. Whether or not such preferences are irrational, insensitive, inconsiderate, or downright racist or sexist, they are part and parcel of who we are. Outside the political world, common sense tells us that no one is *owed* marriage, a job, a friend, or any other relationship.

Although these inner instincts and passions are indeed who we are, we generally keep less tolerant feelings under wraps. The frontal cerebral cortex is our "good housekeeping" management system, keeping in check most inappropriate impulses and temporary pleasures triggered by the amygdala.[2] It restrains us from proposing marriage at the

---

[1]Robert Sapolsky, *Biology and Human Behavior: The Neurological Origins of Individuality*, 2nd ed. (The Teaching Company).

[2]Ibid.

first tinge of attraction or punching someone with whom we disagree. Our frontal cortex, not fully developed until around twenty-five years of age, is the long-term pleasure seeker that will generally (hopefully!) override our short-term impulses, risky choices, and outbursts fostered by the amygdala.

Bigotry, racism, and homophobia are certainly not signs of virtue or good character; however, they are passive feelings that do not constitute aggression in themselves. Physical aggression against those peacefully minding their own business is inhumane and uncivil, no matter the feelings from which it stems. Moreover, there are no greater aggressive displays of bigotry, racism, and homophobia than those taking place in the political arena where laws prohibiting as well as enforcing associations paint a sordid historical picture. Laws that prohibit, compel, or license the association of persons of a given gender, kinship, race, nationality, trade, title, religion, or age demonstrate the extent to which political democracy delves into personal affairs. In the nonpolitical world, relationships and associations are voluntary, joint ventures.

There are no stronger or more peaceful means for bonding humans of different cultures than the synergism of open markets, where interactive trading is neither forced nor prohibited. Such trading and bonding were well underway some thirty thousand years ago, with further evidence of trading as early as one hundred thousand years ago. Trading goods also engendered the transfer of ideas between nomadic and settled tribes. As Julia Allison described the process, "They [nomads] functioned as the human equivalent of bees, fostering the 'cross-pollination of cultures and ideas' among incongruent societies."[3]

As trading gained popularity, cities emerged as grand trading centers, bringing people of different cultures, talents,

---

[3] Julia Allison, "Nomadic versus Settled Societies in World History," JuliaAllison.com. December 2002, http://juliaallison.com/nomadic-vs-settled-societies-in-world-history/.

and specialties together. This emerging division of labor began to replace self-sufficiency, where previously people had to produce for themselves everything they needed to survive. Farmers could concentrate on growing crops, which they traded for clothes, utensils, and tools. Merchants, serving as intermediaries, facilitated these exchanges. Cities grew and prospered, with merchants developing pragmatic rules of conduct based primarily on ostracizing those who failed to meet their promises.[4] Eventually, rulers entered the scene — accompanied by taxes, bribes, and wars — gradually reducing many of those once-popular, synergistic trade centers into posts of abandoned edifices. As rulers increased their stranglehold over the trading activity of people in one area, people migrated to less oppressive areas, as remains the pattern today.

Laws that interfere with the natural association of people simply exacerbate animosities and harmful discrimination. As mentioned earlier, pitting people of different color, wealth, and gender against each other to gain political power is sufficient reason in itself to disavow the political process. The history of legal restrictions on immigration, land ownership, and hiring people of selected ancestries is a sad commentary on politics in the United States and other countries.[5,6]

Equal Employment Opportunity (EEO) laws invite lawyers to file frivolous claims, because the cost of burdensome discovery and defense, coupled with ambiguities in

---

[4]Matt Ridley, *The Rational Optimist: How Prosperity Evolves* (New York: Harper Perennial, 2011).

[5]Kevin R. Johnson, "Race, the Immigration Laws, and Domestic Race Relations: A 'Magic Mirror' into the Heart of Darkness," *Indiana Law Journal* 73, no. 4 (1998).

[6]The Supreme Court upheld the Chinese Exclusion Act and Scott Act in *Chae Chan Ping v. United States* (1889). It declared that "the power of exclusion of foreigners [is] an incident of sovereignty belonging to the Government of the United States as a part of those sovereign powers delegated by the Constitution."

the law, generally force employers to settle.[7] Ironically, an employer accused of discrimination in firing an employee probably did not discriminate when hiring that person: yet after being extorted, the employer will be apt to undetectably modify future considerations when hiring someone.

Laws that prohibit discrimination are inherently discriminatory when applied to only one side of a prospective or existing association. For instance, an employer is prohibited from discriminating when hiring or firing someone, yet a person seeking or quitting a job is free to do so.[8] Applying such laws to only one party of a contractual arrangement requires selective discrimination between the parties. Such a double standard is akin to allowing one partner to discriminate in selecting or divorcing a spouse while prohibiting the other from doing the same. Relationships are mutual arrangements that are only hindered when one or the other party is prohibited from expressing his or her preferences.

People shielded from discrimination likely wonder whether their acceptance by others is sincere or staged. When they receive praise, they will be unsure whether it is merited or legally compelled. The most destructive social impact of antidiscrimination laws is fostering an attitude that everyone is *owed* respect, irrespective of whether it has been earned. The common-sense *earning* of respect becomes instead a *demand* for it as an entitlement.

Political censorship has muzzled the free expression of thoughts to the point where any utterance can be claimed to offend someone. Aside from actual slander, adults claiming to be offended by what others think and say about them are either insecure in their own self-image or,

---

[7] Only 6 percent of those filing employment-discrimination lawsuits in federal courts reach trial, where their chances of winning are only one in three. http://www.abajournal.com/files/employment.pdf.

[8] Laws that prohibit discrimination pertain to age, disability, equal pay/compensation, genetic information, harassment, national origin, pregnancy, race/color, religion, retaliation, sex, and sexual harassment.

very likely, simply using the law to extort or stop someone who dares to openly oppose their political agenda.

In today's world of politics, celebrities live a precarious life and must always be on guard for fear that their words may trigger an onslaught from a so-called offended group, with their picketers, readily-prepared posters, and hackneyed phrases. Offensive speech claims have gone beyond mere comments about gender, race, and religion to attack any expression, gesture, or object that someone considers offensive — either to themselves or others.[9]

In his book *Kindly Inquisitors*, Jonathan Rauch states:

> Impelled by the notions that science is oppression and criticism is violence, the central regulation of debate and inquiry is returning to respectability — this time in a humanitarian disguise. In America, in France, in Austria, and Australia and elsewhere, the old principle of the Inquisition is being revived: people who hold wrong and hurtful opinions should be punished for the good of society. If they cannot be put in jail, then they should lose their jobs, be subjected to organized campaigns of vilification, be made to apologize, be pressed to recant. If government cannot do the punishing, then private institutions and pressure groups — thought vigilantes, in effect — should do it.[10]

On university campuses, politically driven students can muzzle spokespersons and professors from expressing any views incompatible with their own. In politics, demeaning

---

[9] George Leef, "John Leo on the Political Correctness Mania at Marquette," September 30, 2014, http://www.nationalreview.com/phi-beta-cons/389148/john-leo-political-correctness-mania-marquette-george-leef.

[10] Jonathan Rauch, *Kindly Inquisitors: The New Attacks on Free Thought* (Chicago: University of Chicago Press, 1993), p. 6.

such spokespersons and staging protests replace reasoned and persuasive arguments to refute ideas. Consider how quickly student vigilantes would protest someone scheduled to speak about the negative effect of antidiscrimination laws, and how they would instead welcome another who would speak about their positive effect. They would likely not recognize such preferences to be discriminatory nor sense either their own hate when attacking hate mongers or their lack of tolerance of those they claim to be intolerant.

When protesters prohibit speakers from expressing a belief considered contrary to theirs, they display serious doubts about their own convictions. If they were truly convinced about the validity of their beliefs, they would welcome scrutiny as an opportunity to showcase them and demonstrate the invalidity of the opposing view. Using force to silence those who don't share a belief is an obvious indication that one's belief is fallacious.

Aside from their inconsistencies and insecurities, protesters ignore the real world, where censorship and prohibition only increase curiosity. Censor a book, and there's a good chance it will become a bestseller; prohibit the sale of alcohol, and bootleggers and speakeasies pop up all over the place.

The common-sense perspective that prevails outside the political world rests on the notion that no one owes you anything, including good feelings — that you earn the respect of others and what others think about you is their business. Outside the political world, good manners, tolerance, decency, and common courtesy are encouraged and emulated, but not decreed. Such conduct must emerge from the volitional interaction of people: it is counterproductive to use dicta and punishment to command good behavior and conformity to another's prescribed standards. The clergy could provide good guidance in these matters, but unfortunately, many engage in politics and endorse laws that condone, and even encourage, conduct contrary to the ideals they otherwise preach.

In *Ethnic America*, Thomas Sowell points to nine ethnic groups, recounting their struggles as new immigrants and their eventual assimilation into the American mosaic.[11] Intergroup animosities slowly (though very rapidly on the evolutionary scale) declined. Jews, who had been excluded from many top university faculties, ultimately came to be overrepresented in them. Professional sports that had once excluded blacks came to be dominated by black athletes. Anti-Asian laws that flourished in California were eventually repealed via referendums. By the mid-twentieth century, the intermarriages of people of Irish, Polish, German, Italian, and Japanese ancestries had increased to around 50 percent.[12] I was born in 1929 and grew up in an Italian neighborhood in Indiana, where virtually all my aunts and uncles married Italians. However, their children — my cousins — for the most part married non-Italians. I was one of the exceptions when my wife of Italian ancestry and I married in 1953.

Most likely, long before a few millennia pass, intergroup animosities will largely disappear as cultures and races blend into one another and nation states disappear, along with their inherent divisiveness.

---

[11]Thomas Sowell, *Ethnic America: A History* (New York: Basic Books, 1981).

[12]Ibid., p. 9.

6

Tragedy of the Commons and Human Behavior

What is common to the greatest number has the lease care bestowed upon it. Everyone thinks chiefly of his own, hardly at all of the commone Interest.

— Aristotle (*Politics*, Book II, ch.3)

WHY DO PEOPLE BEHAVE THE way they do? The answer to this age-old, fundamental question is essential if someone plans to propose a rule to bring about a peaceful and prosperous community. If we understand why people behave the way they do, we can generally predict how they are apt to behave, given the circumstances. "Tragedy of the commons," or more accurately, "the tragedy of open access," illustrates *how* people behave, given the problem of open access to a limited resource.

Ultimately, everyone behaves in ways they consider in their best interest. Selfishness is the immutable driving force of life. The forces of nature that sculpt the structure of our bodies, hearts, and kidneys are the same that sculpt our behavior.[1] Our brains evolved to regulate behavior to maximize gene replication. In other words, selfishness underlies the traits that determine the proficiency of gene replication. The genes that produce "good" traits leave more copies. In social animals such as ourselves, genes favoring cooperation (a reciprocal mechanism) emerged as a more adaptive trait than did those favoring aggression.

As discussed in chapter 3, cooperators must have mechanisms that perform specific tasks. Cooperation (reciprocation) cannot evolve if an organism lacks reasoning procedures that can effectively detect cheaters (i.e., those who take conditionally offered benefits without providing the promised return). Such individuals would be open to exploitation, and hence their genes selected out. Consequently, we are genetically programmed to cooperate with reciprocators and not with those who do not reciprocate.

There are two general circumstances in which open access to resources can lead to the tragedy of the commons. One is where nature replenishes resources (natural renewable resources) such as off-shore fisheries, forests, open pastures, and underground water basins. In this instance, the given area of a resource is unowned and has unrestricted access, thereby allowing anyone to exploit the resource at will. The other circumstance is where members of a community produce and replenish resources (human renewable resources) such as goods and services. In this instance, the produced resource is or becomes part of a communal pool for appropriation by the members, irrespective of their individual contribution.

Let's first examine how people are apt to behave when faced with a tragedy of the commons in which there is open access to a natural, renewable resource. The dilemma arises when you know (as do others) that when there is unrestricted access to a resource, the rational, self-interest

---

[1]Robert Sapolsky, *Biology and Human Behavior: The Neurological Origins of Individuality*, 2nd ed (The Teaching Company).

choice is to take as much as possible in the here and now because everyone else will be doing the same, but you also know that such rational, individual behavior will not be in your or anyone else's best interest in the long run because it will completely deplete the resource.

The choice people face in such a situation is sometimes equated to the hypothetical prisoner's dilemma,[2] where the rational choice is to not cooperate (i.e., defect). However, the game-theory model of the prisoner's dilemma has several limitations that are not present in real-life decision-making. First, in the prisoner's case, there are only two participants; second, the prisoners cannot talk to each other; third, the rules of the game are inflexible; and fourth, there is only one encounter (episode or game). In the real game of life (on or off the commons), there are multiple participants with ongoing communications, repeated encounters, and the ability to modify strategies (choices) based on results (i.e., trial and error). With these significant differences, people can avoid the tragedy of the commons because everyone involved is selfishly motivated to discover the best strategy to optimize their individual return on investment (time and effort) over the long term.

In her lifelong work, Nobel Laureate Elinor Ostrom (1933–2012) studied such open-access resources and discovered that, notwithstanding the dilemma encountered in a commons, there is a large body of common sense in the world. She found that people, when left to themselves, would sort out rational ways of surviving and getting along. Although the world's arable land, forests, fresh

---

[2]The prisoner's dilemma is a game-theoretic model that posits two prisoners accused of a joint crime who are each given two choices: squeal (defect, "D") on your partner or deny his participation in the crime (cooperate, "C"). The jail sentence each will receive depends on the choices made by both prisoners. They cannot talk to each other. The possible combined choices are CC, CD, DC, and DD. Based on the assigned level of punishment for each outcome, the rational choice for both prisoners is to defect (squeal), yet they would have each received a lesser sentence if they had instead both cooperated (denied the other's participation).

water, and fisheries are all finite, it is possible to share them without depleting them and care for them without fighting. Years of fieldwork by Ostrom and others showed her that humans are not trapped and helpless amid diminishing supplies. She looked at forests in Nepal, irrigation systems in Spain, mountain villages in Switzerland and Japan, and fisheries in Maine and Indonesia. She even, as part of her PhD program at the University of California-Los Angeles, studied the water wars and pumping races going on in the 1950s in her own dry backyard.

Ostrom found that people tended to draw up sensible rules for the use of common-pool resources. Neighbors set boundaries and assigned shares, with each person taking turns to use water or graze cows on a certain meadow. They performed common tasks such as clearing canals or cutting timber together at certain times. Monitors watched out for rule breakers, fining or eventually excluding them. The schemes were mutual and reciprocal, and many had worked well for centuries. Best of all, they were not imposed from above. Ostrom put no faith in governments or large conservation schemes paid for with aid money and crawling with concrete-bearing engineers. Caring for the commons has to be a multiple task organized from the ground up and shaped to cultural norms. It has to be discussed face-to-face and based on trust.[3]

Given the evolutionary biology studies discussed earlier, we should not be surprised to see such cooperative strategies emerge in areas of the commons. We are here because natural selection favored our ancient ancestors whose behavior took advantage of the synergism of cooperation and its lower risk of conflict. The only surprise would be for those in the political world who find the bottom-up emergence of orderly strategies not orchestrated by government to be abnormal. In chapter 8, we

---

[3]"Elinor Ostrom," *Economist*, June 30, 2012, http://www.economist.com/node/21557717.

will see that the bottom-up emergence of order is indeed the norm in nature — genes cooperate with other genes, cells with other cells, and organisms with other organisms in a symbiotic and yet selfish manner — all without a conductor.

Most instructive in Ostrom's studies is the creativity of people trying to solve problems complicated by their own propensity to appropriate as much as possible — and how the varied strategies, while devised independently, have certain common characteristics. The variation in strategies was based on the type of resource, its accessibility, and local customs. The common elements that Ostrom found to be essential for a strategy to be successful were:

- The rules and strategies need to be discovered through a dynamic evolutionary process of trial and error.

- The rules must be devised by those using the resource.

- The users of the resource must be responsible for monitoring and enforcing their rules.

- Most important is the presumption against central planning — the plan must avoid immediate recourse to central regulations that will undermine the incentive for resource users themselves to devise rules. [4]

Governing the Commons[5] by Ostrom is a superb testament to the understanding that can be gained when economists observe in close-up detail how people craft arrangements to solve problems in ways often

---

[4]Ibid.; see remarks by Ostrom, 26–34.

[5]Elinor Ostrom, *Governing the Commons: The Evolution of Institutions for Collective Action* (Cambridge, UK: Cambridge University Press, 2015).

beyond the imagination of textbook theorists. In particular, communities are often able to find stable and effective ways to define the boundaries of a common-pool resource, define the rules for its use, and effectively enforce those rules.[6]

In summary, when people are left to their own devices they are most capable of structuring local rules to which every member agrees to adapt his or her behavior according to a strategy that each finds personally advantageous. Government force is incapable of accomplishing that which volition accomplishes naturally.

Let's now examine how people are apt to behave when the resources produced by members of a community become common-pool resources with open access.

Biologically, we do not behave for the good of the community but rather for the good of ourselves, our kin, according to the degree of relatedness, and others when reciprocity serves our purpose. We cannot behave unselfishly (gene-wise) no matter how much we try or how much we are forced to do so. People will naturally adapt their behavior to optimize their investment of time and effort, given their current circumstances.

A family living independently is well aware that it is solely responsible for its own livelihood. Common sense tells its members that they cannot consume more than they produce. They are naturally motivated to behave prudently to produce and consume accordingly. Cheating is not an option for those living independently.

When joining a community, a family can continue to manage its productive and consumptive behaviors or change them to predatory behavior. The synergistic advantage of living near others will motivate cooperative behavior

---

[6]Elinor Ostrom, with comments by Christina Chang, Mark Pennington and Vlad Tarko, *The Future of the Commons*, November 1, 2012 Institute of Economic Affairs. See comment by Mark Pennington, p. 14.

because reputation and trust are paramount if people want to remain members and gain the benefits of the community. Preying upon your neighbor is a good way to get ostracized from the neighborhood, since cooperation is a *reciprocal* mechanism.

The tragedy of the commons arises when rules are adopted or enforced that prohibit a person from controlling the distribution of that which he or she produces. Absent the ability to withhold goods from those detected as cheaters, predatory behavior becomes the norm within the community. Common sense tells us that if we are unable to ostracize slackers and free riders, we are less apt to behave cooperatively (i.e., reciprocally) because no one wants to be taken for a sucker. As Charles Stangor notes, "The sucker effect occurs when perceiving that one is contributing more to a task than others, lead[ing] individuals to withhold effort as a means of restoring equity and avoiding being taken advantage of."[7]

The tragedy can occur even when the members agree to a communal arrangement. However, the cause of the tragedy (slacking and free riding) will quickly become apparent because we are genetically programmed to detect cheaters. Consequently, the members will be motivated to abandon their communal pooling arrangement and allow each member to control the distribution of that which he or she produces.

Governor William Bradford's account of the Pilgrims of Plymouth exemplifies the tragedy when a communal system is adopted for the production and distribution of goods and services. When each Pilgrim had access to an equal share of the stores produced from the land used in common for growing crops without regard to their personal contribution, the community experienced a dwindling quantity of stores produced. Facing another year

---

[7]Charles Stangor, *Social Groups in Action and Interaction* (New York: Routledge, 2015).

of famine, the communal system was abandoned and replaced with a system that allowed each family to work its own allocated plot and retain or trade whatever it produced. In 1623 — the first year following the change — the community experienced its most abundant harvest, which was and still is celebrated as Thanksgiving.

The diary kept by Governor Bradford is a testament to how people behave given the adoption of rules that run counter to their natural selfish inclinations, particularly where each person must share the product of his or her labor equally among all the community members. Not only did the communal system produce little in resources, it engendered strife and discontent between the members of the small community, even though they all shared a common and strict Christian faith. From the diary of William Bradford, circa 1623:

> *Whille no supply was heard of, neither knew they when they might expecte any. So they begane to thinke how they might raise as much torne [corn] as they could, and obtaine a beter crope then they had done, that they might not still thus languish in miserie. At length, after much debate of things, the Govr (with the advise of the cheefest amongest them) gave way that they should set corve [crops from labor] every man for his owne perticuler, and in that regard trust to them selves; in all other things to goe on in the generall way as before. And so assigned to every family a parcell of land, according to the proportion of their number for that end, only for present use (but made no devission for inheritance), and ranged all boys and youth under some familie. This had very good success; for it made all hands very industrious, so as much more torne was planted then other waise would have bene by any means the Govr or any other could use, and saved him a great deall of trouble,*

and gave farr better contente. The women now wente willingly into the feild, and tooke their litle-ons with them to set torne, which before would aledg weaknes, and inabilitie; whom to have compelled would have bene thought great tiranie and oppression.

The experience that was had in this commone course and condition, tried sundrie years, and that amongst godly and sober men, may well evince the vanitie of that conceite of Platos and other ancients, applauded by some of later times; — that the taking away of propertie, and brining in communitie into a comone wealth, would make them happy and florishing; as if they were wiser then God. For this comunitie (so farr as it was) was found to breed much confusion and discontent, and retard much imployment that would have been to their benefite and comforte. For the yong-men that were most able and fitte for labour and servise did repine that they should spend their time and streingth to worke for other mens wives and children, with out any recompence. The strong, or man of parts, had no more in devission of victails and cloaths, then he that was weake and not able to doe a quarter the other could; this was thought injuestice. The aged and graver men to be ranked and equalised in labours, and victails, cloaths, etc., with the meaner and yonger sorte, thought it some indignite and disrespect unto them. And for mens wives to be commanded to doe servise for other men, as dresing their meate, washing their cloaths, etc., they deemd it a kind of slaverie, neither could many husbands well brooke it. Upon the poynte all being to have alike, and all to doe alike, they thought them selves in the like condition, and ove as good as another; and so, if it did not cut of those relations that God hath set amongest men, yet it did at least much

> *diminish and take of the mutuall respects that*
> *should be preserved amongst them. And would*
> *have bene worse if they had been men of another*
> *condition. Let pone objecte this is mens corrup-*
> *tion, and nothing to the course it selfe. I answer,*
> *seeing all men have this corruption in them,*
> *God in his wisdome saw another course fiter for*
> *them.*[8]

A summarized reading of Bradford's diary:

Because we had not heard of the arrival of any supplies or if any were on the way, we had to think about how we might raise as much corn as possible to obtain a better crop and avoid languishing in misery. After a long debate the Governor (with the advice of the chiefest amongst them) decided to set the crops for each man in particular to own and work. So, every family was assigned a parcel of land according to the family size. This arrangement had very good success; for it made all hands very industrious, so that much more corn was planted than would have been planted otherwise. The women now went willingly to the field and took their little ones with them to help plant corn, whereas before they would allege weakness and inabilities and complain about being oppressed.

The experience we had was contrary to the conceit of Plato and other ancients that the taking away of property and bringing into the community a common wealth would make them happy and flourishing; as if they were wiser than God. For the community was found to breed much confusion and discontent, and retard much employment that would have been to their benefit and comfort. The young men who were more able and fit for labor and ser-vice complained that they should spend time and strength working for the other men's wives and children without compensation. The strong men thought it an injustice that

---

[8]Paul Solman, "Communism, Capitalism and the Third Thanksgiving," PBS, November 22, 2012.

they would receive the same share of food and clothes that those who were weaker and only able to do a quarter of the work received. The older and graver men found that the equal ranking in labor, food, and clothes with that of the meaner and younger ones to be indignant and disrespectful. For men's wives to be commanded to do service for other men such as dressing their meat and washing their clothes, etc., they deemed to be a kind of slavery and their husbands could not tolerate it. The point of all having to be alike and do alike they thought of themselves in the like condition and only as good as another. It took away the mutual respect that should be preserved amongst them.

Rules that ignore the biological nature of behavior simply invite tragedy. The disastrous consequences that follow the adoption of rules counter to man's biological nature may be unintended, but are nevertheless predictable. There are annals of tragic, unintended consequences that should give anyone pause before issuing a rule designed to improve social welfare. Simply going about adopting and enforcing one rule after another, hoping one will actually produce good consequences, without bothering to understand the immutable selfish nature of human behavior, is characteristic of the inhumane world of politics and government.

The tragedy of communal access to human resources is exemplified in a political democracy, where free riders have equal say about the distribution of resources as do those who produce them. The growing number of those on the dole in the United States reached sixty-seven million, or 20 percent of the population, in 2012 — an annual welfare distribution of $2.5 trillion.[9] Should anyone with

---

[9]Post Staff Report, "On the Dole: A Fifth of All Americans," *New York Post,* February 13, 2013. https://nypost.com/2012/02/13/on-the-dole-a-fifth-of-all-americans. William Beach and Patrick Tyrrell, "The 2012 Index of Dependence on Government," Heritage Foundation February 8, 2012.

even a modicum of common sense be surprised to see such figures?

The empirical evidence surrounding open access to natural resources demonstrates the creative ability of people when left to their own devices to harmoniously solve their social problems and the disruptive effect of external people trying to solve social problems for them with top-down dicta and force. The tragedy that sensible people are able to avoid when left alone is the very tragedy governments perpetuate.

7

Obedience to Authority

The disappearance of a sense of responsibility is the most far-reaching consequence of submission to authority.

— Stanley Milgram (1933–84)

Those who can make you believe absurdities can make you commit atrocities.

— Voltaire (1694–1778)

WHEN I ASKED YOU EARLIER (in chapter 4) to imagine a scene with John Rawls knocking on his neighbor's door to assert his claim about fairness and justice, we both knew he would never have considered carrying out such a repugnant stunt. I have no doubt he was a dignified gentleman who treated those around him with great respect, as most likely are others who propose laws that authorize and order actions they would not for a second consider carrying out personally on their neighbors. Where do these individuals find the justification to bridge the divide between their private moral judgments and their public ones? Those who take these dichotomous positions are certainly not schizophrenic or psychopathic; nevertheless, they seem to feel comfortable and justified endorsing public acts they would find reprehensible if carried out within their own inner circles.

Stanley Milgram's renowned Yale University experiment highlights the powerful human tendency to obey authority.[1] Conducted in his laboratory in 1963, the experiment studied the range of destructive obedience. Using the pretext of a memory experiment, it consisted of ordering a naïve volunteer "teacher" to administer increasingly severe "electric shocks" to someone acting as a student when the supposed student failed to answer questions correctly. The electric panel of levers, switches, and dials was a façade, and the cries from the hidden "student" — commensurate with the panel's indicated voltage levels — were fake.

While not everyone in the experiment carried out these orders, and some even protested, 60 percent of the participants did fully "shock" the supposed student. Unfortunately, some participants who obeyed the order at the highest level of voltage later suffered mental stress for having done so, even though they learned at the end of their sessions that they had not actually harmed anyone.

As part of the experiment, Milgram varied the distance between the participant and the hidden student and discovered that the closer the student was to the participant, the less obedient the participant became. He also tested the level of obedience when the participant was joined by two others (actors) who refused to comply when he ordered them to administer the highest shock. In these cases, only 10 percent of the participants were willing to administer the highest shock, indicating a reluctance to obey a repulsive command when joined by others who refused to obey.

Milgram's experiment took place the year following the trial, conviction, and execution of Adolf Eichmann for his part in the Holocaust. At his trial, Eichmann did not

---

[1]Stanley Milgram, *Obedience to Authority: An Experimental View* (New York: Harper Perennial Modern Classics, 2009).

deny his acts and proudly claimed to have been obedient to his superiors, following orders and the law as any loyal citizen should do. Hannah Arendt recounts the trial in her book *Eichmann in Jerusalem: A Report on the Banality of Evil*:

> To each count Eichmann pleaded: "Not guilty in the sense of the indictment."
>
> In what sense then did he think he was guilty? In the long cross-examination of the accused, according to him "the longest ever known," neither the defense nor the prosecution nor, finally, any of the three judges ever bothered to ask him this obvious question. His lawyer, Robert Servatius of Cologne, hired by Eichmann and paid by the Israeli government, answered the question in a press interview: "Eichmann feels guilty before God, not before the law," but this answer remained without confirmation from the accused himself. The defense would apparently have preferred him to plead not guilty on the grounds that under the then existing Nazi legal system he had not done anything wrong, that what he was accused of were not crimes but "acts of state," over which no other state has jurisdiction (par in parem imperium non habet.), that it had been his duty to obey and that, in Servatius' words, he had committed acts "for which you are decorated if you win and go to the gallows if you lose.[2]

Eichmann was examined by a court-appointed psychiatrist and psychologist who found him to be quite normal,[3]

---

[2]Hannah Arendt, *Eichmann in Jerusalem: Report on the Evil* (New York: Viking Press, 1963), p. 14.

[3]According to Jos Brunner, the finding by the psychiatrist that Eichmann was normal may have been influenced by the prosecution's attempt to

eliciting a fear that maybe we all have a latent tendency to obey authority and laws that can, in certain circumstances, override our inherent common sense of decency. In Eichmann's case, it wasn't a matter of him facing dire consequences if he had not taken on the job: he freely volunteered to do it.

When giving lectures on his experiment, Milgram was astonished to discover that students were aghast, proclaiming they would never behave in such a way — yet months later, they served in the military and carried out orders that made shocking a victim seem pallid.[4] We all like to consider ourselves above such rank obedience, yet there exists within us a strong tendency to obey those in authority, even when our deeper feelings tell us that what we are doing is not quite right. Milgram argues that once we have accepted the right of an authority to direct our actions, we relinquish responsibility to him or her and allow that person to define what is right and wrong for us.[5] This "obedience to authority," as Milgram calls it, is a frightening part of our nature:

> Ordinary people, simply doing their jobs, and without any particular hostility on their part, can become agents in a terrible destructive process. Moreover, even when the destructive effects of their work become patently clear, and they are asked to carry out actions incompatible with fundamental standards of morality, relatively few

preclude the defense from pleading insanity. See José Brunner, "Eichmann's Mind: Psychological, Philosophical, and Legal Perspectives," *Theoretical Inquiries in Law* 1, no. 2 (2000).

[4]Michael Shermer, *The Science of Good and Evil: Why People Cheat, Gossip, Care, Share, and Follow the Golden Rule* (New York: Times Books, 2004), p. 73.

[5]American Psychological Association, "Obeying and Resisting Malevolent Orders," *Research in Action*, May 25, 2004.

people have the resources needed to resist authority.[6]

There is ample literature on the strong propensity of humans to obey authority and carry out directives and orders they would otherwise find repugnant. However, whom, if anyone, are people obeying when they issue orders for others to carry out? Political democracy appears to convey, by way of public consensus, an authoritative directive for an order issuer to dutifully obey in the same way an order taker obeys an issuer. The person issuing an order transfers personal responsibility for his conduct to a consensus, while the person carrying out the order transfers personal responsibility of his conduct to the issuer.

Every day, heads of state issue hundreds of intrusive and abusive orders for their bureaucratic minions to dutifully enforce. Imbued with power, otherwise placid people sadly turn into headstrong bullies who obediently trample over the affairs and lives of their fellow men. Without the incessant political propaganda, however, the task of these empowered minions to successfully enforce these orders would be insurmountable. As discussed earlier, we are conditioned from childhood to believe that being a good citizen requires our obedience to political authority.

IRS agents are well known for their heavy-handed, heartless way of intimidating people, which destroys livelihoods and businesses, and even causes numerous suicides.[7] Some years ago, the young man who serviced my home pool committed suicide because of an IRS threat. This exemplifies how political democracy can desensitize a person to become just such a terrifying and feared member of society.

---

[6]Stanley Milgram, "The Perils of Obedience," *Harper's*, December 1973.

[7]Jack W. Wade Jr., and Jack Shafer, "Confessions of an IRS Agent," April 1983, http://www.abolishirs.org/3_3.html; Richard Yancey, *Confessions of a Tax Collector: One Man's Tour of Duty Inside the IRS* (New York: Harper Perennial, 2004).

The following is a segment of a speech, "The Uniqueness of Humans," given by neuroendocrinologist Robert Sapolsky to Stanford University students on Class Day 2009. His portrayal of obedience to government authority shows the degree to which the most caring humans can be desensitized to conduct themselves in the most abhorrent ways:

> Every day, outside of Las Vegas, there are people who get up in the morning, and they are rushing off to work, and their spouse reminds them to pick up the dry cleaning on the way home, and they say goodbye to their kids, and they rush out, and they get caught in traffic, and they're all anxious they're going to be late at work, and they luck out and get a good parking spot and get to work and sit down in a flight simulator and what they spend the day doing is operating a drone bomber in Iraq that drops bombs and kills people. This is at Nellis Air Force Base. People sitting there spending their work days operating drone bombers on the other side of the world, and at the end of the day, having finished your day doing that, you get up and rush off because you want to be there on time for your daughter's ballet performance, and you hug her afterward, and you can't believe it's possible to love someone that much. And the next day you sit in this dark room and kill people on the other side of the planet. And there's nothing out there in the animal world that has a precedent for that. Not surprisingly, apparently the rate of psychiatric problems among people who spend their days doing this is also unprecedented.[8]

---

[8]Robert Sapolsky, "The Uniqueness of Humans" speech, Class Day

Acquiescence to the commands of an authority that are only mildly objectionable is often — as in Milgram's experiments — the beginning of a step-by-step, escalating process of entrapment. The farther people move along the continuum of increasingly destructive acts, the harder it is to extract themselves from the commanding authority's grip, because to do so is to confront the fact that the earlier acts of compliance were wrong.[9]

By endorsing the enforcement of a law considered too repugnant to personally enforce against a neighbor, one authorizes others to obediently enforce that law as his or her proxy.

Stanford University 2009, https://www.youtube.com/watch?v=hrCV u25wQ5s.

[9] American Psychological Association, "Obeying and Resisting Malevolent Orders," *Research in Action*, May 25, 2004.

8

Complexity, Adaption, and Order: Visualizing the Invisible Hand

Yet this government never of itself furthered any enterprise, but by the alacrity with which it got out of its way.

— Henry David Thoreau (1817–62)

Do not think of what you see but see what it took to produce what you see.

— Benoit Mandelbrot (1924–2010)

Life is not only stranger than we imagine; life is stranger than we can imagine.

— John Haldane (1954–)

WHEN WE ENVISION TWO PEOPLE interacting, we can easily picture an orderly scene. But as we add more people to that image, the orderliness becomes more difficult to envision. We can easily sense in our duo scene that each person is acting orderly, because we likely see ourselves as one of them, knowing that cooperation is a more efficacious course of action in our pursuit of well-being. Not only would we not sense a need for a central planner to direct and enforce our interactions, we would also consider the idea absurd and, if imposed on us, downright disorderly.

Irrespective of the size of the group, whether a nation of millions or a planet of billions, each person is an individual actor, genetically guided to act based on the same local, self-serving, simple rules that are no different from those in our duo scene. "Tit for tat," "the Golden Rule," and "live and let live" are all normal, adaptive, neighborhood rules of human conduct, the essence of which are cooperating/ competing/ostracizing algorithms.

Robert Axelrod conducted two computer tournaments to identify the winning rule in a game theory setting. The objective was to gain a deeper understanding of how to perform well in such a setting. The winning rule in both tournaments was "tit for tat," in which a player cooperates on the first move and then does whatever the other player did on the previous move. The results show that there is value in being somewhat forgiving while at the same time not being the first to defect — as well as the importance of being provocable.[1] In evolutionary jargon, "tit for tat" drove the other rules into extinction.

The natural orderliness of unordered interactions has been observed for centuries. One of the earliest records comes from Chuang-tzu (369–286 BC) who noted, "Good order results spontaneously when things are let alone." In the eighteenth century, Adam Smith observed that individuals acting in their own self-interest lead to an orderly and prosperous society as if led by an "invisible hand." A century later, Charles Darwin (1809–82) observed that organisms of myriad structures neatly fit into their surrounding environment as if selected by nature.

The new field of chaos theory, which has gained the more descriptive names of "systems theory," "complexity theory," and "theory of self-organizing systems," gives us

---

[1]Robert Axelrod, "More Effective Choice in the Prisoner's Dilemma," *Journal of Conflict Resolution* 24, no. 3 (1980): 379–403.

a deeper understanding of how living and nonliving matter naturally form orderly systems and structures of enormous complexity. This new way of looking at and understanding the world comes from the perspective of a system, rather than only from an atomistic or reductionist perspective. Even when we know the properties of the individual parts of or participants in the system, we cannot accurately predict the outcome of their interactions because it will not equal the sum of their respective properties. The characteristic of such a system is that the whole is greater than the sum of its parts because the system has properties that are not possessed by any of its parts.

The crux of this exciting and revolutionary science is that a social order of unimaginable complexity emerges from simple but profound local rules without any top-down directives.

> Social scientist, Scott Page provides us with a brilliant distillation of complexity theory: "An actor in a complex system controls almost nothing but influences almost everything. Attempts to intervene may be akin to poking a tiger with a stick."[2]

The idea of spontaneous order that results from randomly interacting organic and inorganic parts without a designer or director is counterintuitive. This new science is just that; we can't easily envision it, and equally frustrating is the impossibility of predicting long-term outcomes while knowing the initial conditions, the properties of the parts, and understanding the process. We are inclined to believe that order requires a designer, but design does not need an interacting designer — it is an inherent part of the universe.[3]

---

[2]Scott E. Page, *Understanding Complexity* (The Teaching Company), Lecture 12.

[3]Richard Dawkins provides an exhaustive explanation of how a natural feedback system can create biological complexity in his masterpiece *The*

When we imagine millions of people interacting, we are overwhelmed by the enormity and complexity of that scene and are compelled to conclude that top-down intervention is necessary — that someone needs to be in charge to rule and orchestrate all of us — otherwise, all hell will break loose. Secondly, we intuitively sense that the more complex a system is, the more complex the rules must be to effectively bring about and maintain order. Thirdly, we naturally assume that the greater the number of participants in a system, the greater the potential for disorder and chaos, thus requiring a greater degree of top-down orchestration. Finally, we assume that the more diverse the participants are in the system, the lower the probability of a successful and orderly system will be.

Remarkably, this new science dispels all four of these notions by demonstrating how orderly systems naturally emerge and evolve from randomly interacting parts.

- First, the order and complexity we see in all of nature's systems emerge from bottom-up, local rules without being guided by a master or a master plan. Feedback following an act will guide actors to either repeat or modify future acts. Top-down enforcement of rules that interfere with the emergence of order that stems from self-serving, volitional adaption to local circumstances simply squanders energy to offset the disorderly intrusions. Additionally, imposed political rules and regulations hamper the natural ability of people to quickly adapt to changing conditions in their attempt to optimize utility.

- Second, complexity emerges from simple, local, neighborhood rules; generally, the simpler the rule,

---

Blind Watchmaker: Why the Evidence of Evolution Reveals a Universe without Design (New York: W.W. Norton, 1986).

the more successful and orderly the outcome.[4] Tit for tat is an example of such a rule that most of us naturally employ in our acquisition of resources and pursuit of mating opportunities.

- Third, as discussed earlier, the bonding of people of different cultures is best accomplished through trade. With ever more participants, there is a greater potential for innovative individuals to bring exceptional ideas, products, and services to the marketplace, thereby attracting and bonding an even larger array of diverse traders. The benefits gained by each trading participant will engender an interdependency that will make conflict counter to their own self-interest. As such, state tariffs and import restrictions are as disorderly as they are uneconomical.

- Finally, without diversity, markets and societies are worthless; the synergistic benefit of markets is realized only when people of different skills and preferences interact. According to Scott Page: Progress depends as much on our collective differences as it does on our individual IQ scores. Diverse groups of problem solvers outperformed the groups of the best individuals at solving complex problems. The reason: the diverse groups got stuck less often than the smart individuals, who tended to think similarly.[5] Diversity also tends to diminish social disorder because individuals have different thresholds of

[4]Robert Sapolsky, "Human Behavior Biology," *Stanford University,* 150/250, Spring 2010, "Chaos and Reductionism" (Lecture 21) https://www.youtube.com/watch?v=_njf8jwEGRo; and "Emergence and Complexity" (Lecture 22) https://www.youtube.com/watch?v=o_Zu-WbX-CyE.

[5]Scott E. Page, *The Difference: How the Power of Diversity Creates Better Groups, Firms, Schools, and Societies* (Princeton, NJ: Princeton University Press, 2008), p. 26.

reacting to an event. For example, people may rush out of a building if they see others doing so, but only when the number of people they see exceeds their individual threshold. As such, the mass exit may never even begin if just one person rushes out. Bees are an excellent example of the benefits of such diversity: they maintain the temperature of their hive at 86°F and can sense whether it is too hot or too cold. However, each bee does so at a different temperature. Some bees, sensing the hive as too hot at a lower temperature than others do, will leave, flap their wings outside the hive to cool it off, and then return. Other bees, with a higher temperature threshold, will stay put. If bees were not diverse in their temperature sensing, they would all leave and rejoin the hive at the same time, and the temperature would fluctuate widely.

This new science addresses the nonlinear systems of nature, where the output is not directly proportional to the input. This view is a major departure from the reductionist or atomistic approach to science that is the mainstay of scientific literature and studies. The scientific method, dating back to the seventeenth century, in essence involves observing a phenomenon, forming a causal hypothesis, extrapolating that hypothesis, and continually testing it to either validate or invalidate it. This method assumes a deterministic world where phenomena are potentially predictable. Based on this school of science, all complex systems in nature can be understood through the nature of their parts because the whole is simply the sum of its parts. Accordingly, the ability to predict a system's future state should improve commensurate with the increased understanding of the nature of its parts in its current state. The reductionist view of nature also presumes that a small change in a current state will likewise result in a small change in its future state.

No matter how deeply scientists delved into the workings of a system's parts, they were continually confronted with frustrating discrepancies and variations in the outcome. Unexpected discrepancies were attributed to mathematical errors, instrument failure or inadequacies, or simply so-called noise. However, despite improved instruments and refined mathematics, these discrepancies continued to exist. In short, the deeper the reductive search, the more reductive scientists must become.

With discrepancies at every level of resolution, a few scientists eventually concluded that maybe what they observed were not discrepancies but rather inherent features of nature that could not be reduced to their parts. This new, non-reductive science was and remains a bit too unorthodox for many scientists. The late physicist Michel Baranger, for example, initially thought this new science was an affront to everything he and most scientists understood. However, he eventually succumbed to the realization that nature is not a reductive, schematic system. In *The End of Certainty*, Nobel Laureate Ilya Prigogine (1917–2003) contends that determinism is no longer a viable scientific belief: "The more we know about our universe, the more difficult it becomes to believe in determinism."[6] This view is a major departure from the approaches of Isaac Newton and Albert Einstein and their theories, which are expressed as linear deterministic equations. According to Prigogine, determinism loses its explanatory power in the face of irreversibility and instability. He notes numerous examples, among which are evolution and the emergence of life.

In a nonlinear system, we can predict events accurately more or less only one generation at a time, each with a high probability of accuracy, but the accuracy level diminishes over time because the impact of the slightest perturbation or error magnifies exponentially. The time horizon for predicting future events varies depending on the system. In some systems, e.g., electrical, this horizon may be milliseconds, while in others, such as weather, it

---

[6]Ilya Prigogine, *The End of Certainty* (New York: Free Press, 1997).

may be days or even millions of years, as with the solar system.[7]

No matter how sensitive the instruments, how meticulous the observations, or how precise the mathematics, the exponential growth of an unavoidable error and of chance will overwhelm the ability to accurately predict beyond a given period. By either lowering our standards or improving our initial measurement, however, we can always increase the predictable time period. The problem with predictability in a nonlinear system is that if you want to double, triple, or quadruple the predictable time period and maintain the same level of accuracy, you need to work 10, 100, or 1,000 times harder, respectively.[8] In other words, if you want to obtain the same level of predictable accuracy for a ten-day period as a one-day period, you need to increase the preciseness of your initial measurements one billion times.

The "butterfly effect," a term coined by meteorologist Edward Lorenz (1917–2008), metaphorically describes the amplifying effect of a minor wind disturbance such as the flapping of a butterfly's wings causing a major hurricane at a future time in a far-off place.[9] As a pioneer of chaos theory, Lorenz demonstrates why weather predictions will never be accurate for more than a couple of weeks out, irrespective of the increased sensitivity of our instruments and the amount of data collected. In these systems, Lorenz sees order masquerading as randomness. This rapid exponential amplification of a minor event is the trademark of chaos.

Many married couples have likely played a game in which they recall the least significant happenstance that

---

[7]Steven Strogatz, *Chaos as Disorder: The Butterfly Effect* (The Teaching Company), Lecture 6.

[8]Steven Strogatz, *Sync: How Order Emerges from Chaos in the Universe, Nature, and Daily Life* (Hachette Books, 2004), p. 190.

[9]James Glieck, *Chaos, Making of a New Science* (Penguin Books, 2008), ch. 1.

led to their meeting — for instance, "if it hadn't rained that day," "if I hadn't missed the bus," "if we hadn't bumped into each other in the hallway," etc. Or consider the sequencing of so-called butterfly occurrences that led to your parents' matchup and the resulting matchup of the two gametes that became you. As Steven Strogatz points out, while Lorenz is credited with the term "butterfly effect," the realization that little events can have major consequences is likely an ancient observation.

As in all natural complex systems, there are no organizers, orchestrators, or planners to guide the process because there are no blueprints or plans to follow. Even if some parts of a system are disrupted or removed, the remaining parts will reconfigure and reestablish the functions of the system without any central authority controlling them. For example, each ant colony has a given ratio of worker, warrior, and forager ants, depending on the species. Remove or destroy a portion of that colony, and within hours, the ratio of workers, warriors, and foragers will reestablish itself without a central authority. Somehow, these relationships give rise to changes in the physiological development of the ants: warrior ants become much bigger than forager ants, which are bigger than worker ants.[10]

This self-organizing property of the ant colony, like that of other social animals, gives the intuitive appearance that the animals have a plan, or at least some individual animal has a plan. However, that is not the case. There is no plan or design to know. The future state of a system emerges from the interaction of its parts and participants using simple, local, *if/then* rules without any participants knowing what will eventually emerge from the sum of their actions. The internet is a testament to the unimaginable self-organizing complexity of a system that in just

---

[10]Steven Goldman, *Great Scientific Ideas That Changed the World* (The Teaching Company), Lecture 34.

twenty-five years has grown to include and connect half the people of the world.

Knowing the chemical properties of each part will not provide insight into the resulting outcome of their association. Take, for example, the elements sodium and chlorine — both are toxic, but together they organize to form common table salt, which has none of the properties of its parts and cannot be predicted by knowing the properties of each part. Likewise, DNA, whether of a tree, an insect, or a human, contains four bases (adenine, cytosine, guanine, and thymine), with the sequencing making the difference. The amazing structure of an embryo that emerges from two interacting cells provides insight into nature's inherent bottom-up, self-organizing system.

Yaneer Bar-yam writes:

> It is generally believed that the design of plant or animal physiology is contained within the nuclear DNA of the cells. DNA is often called the blueprint for the biological organism. However, it is clear that DNA does not function like an architect's blueprint because the information does not represent the structure of the physiology in a direct way — there is no homunculus there. DNA specifies the interaction between a cell and its environment, including cells in its vicinity, as well as the internal functioning of the cell.[11]

Stephen Wolfram, author of *A New Kind of Science*, suggests there is strong evidence that the level of complexity of individual parts of organisms has not changed much in at least several hundred million years.[12] In other words, the

---

[11]Yaneer Bar-yam, *Dynamics of Complex Systems* (Studies in Nonlinearity) (Westview Press, 1997), p. 622.

[12]Stephen Wolfram, *A New Kind of Science* (Champaign, IL: Wolfram Media, 2002), p. 389.

building blocks used for structuring a biological organism have remained basically the same, with only their arrangement and quantity producing the differences between one organism and another. For instance, the neurons of a fly, chimpanzee, or human look the same, with only the quantity making the difference in each animal's cognitive ability.

According to Wolfram: "Incredibly simple rules that produce incredibly complicated behavior is a very robust and very general phenomenon of nature. It has always been a mystery how nature could manage apparently so effortlessly to produce so much that seems to us so complex; it's as though nature has some secret that allows it to make things so much more complex than we humans can normally build."[13] He suggests that nature is a system of active cells, each sampling a large array of possible rules. What we then see is how those rules play out. The cells that hit upon viable rules are the only ones that can produce organs and organisms able to survive in the given environment in which we find them. The harsher the environment, the fewer the rules that are viable, and thus fewer structural designs can potentially emerge. We can determine whether a rule is viable only by letting it play out. In other words, we cannot determine the viability of a rule *a priori*.

Symbiosis at both the cellular and organism levels is similar: cells cooperate with neighboring cells, as do organisms with neighboring organisms, in a mutual self-serving social network. Symbiotic behavior of both cells and organisms emerges without any superior cell or organism ordering such behavior. Despite the "selfishness" of genes discussed earlier, the optimal way for a gene to replicate is to join other replicators in building cells, organs, and organisms that serve each replicator. In the human genome, 1,195 genes cooperate to produce the heart, 2,164 genes team up

---

[13]Stephen Wolfram, "Computing a Theory of All Knowledge," lecture, TED2010, February 2010, http://www.ted.com/talks/stephen_wolfram_computing_a_theory_of_everything?language=en.

to make a white blood cell, and 3,195 are responsible for the brain, but no gene or cell is in charge of the process.[14] Each of the ten thousand pacemaker cells in the human heart beats independently when isolated in a Petri dish, but when joined with other pacemaker cells, all will beat in unison after only a few days — without any one cell orchestrating the beat.

Such self-synchronization is common in nature, including that found in inanimate structures.[15] For example, two or more similar pendulums on the same shelf, each swinging independently and out of sync, will slowly and automatically synchronize their swings in unison. When people in an audience are asked to clap in unison, they will do so spontaneously within just a few seconds without a single person leading the pace. A school of fish or flock of birds will move abruptly in a synchronized, choreographic pattern, yet no one fish or bird is directing that movement. Instead, each is acting individually based on feedback from its nearest neighbor, thus displaying as a whole a cooperative, rhythmic flow of beauty without a conductor.

Cosmides and Tooby, both noted evolutionary psychologists, describe why top-down institutional planning cannot replace bottom-up, individual decision-making in bringing about social welfare:

> Significantly, the human mind was intensely selected to evolve mechanisms to evaluate its own welfare, and is so equipped by natural selection to compute and represent its own array of preferences in exquisite and often inarticulable detail. The array of n-dimensional rankings that

---

[14]Jurgen Appelo, *Management 3.0: Leading Agile Developers, Developing Agile Leaders* (Addison–Wesley Professional, 2011), p. 262.

[15]Strogatz, *Sync*; Steven Strogatz, "The Science of Sync," lecture, TED 2004, February 2004, http://www.ted.com/talks/steven_strogatz_on_sync? language=en. Filmed, February 2004.

inhabits our motivational systems is too rich to be communicated to others or represented by them, which is one reason displacing value guided decision making to remote institutions systematically damages social welfare. Under a system of private exchange, this richness need not be communicated or understood by anyone else — its power is harnessed effectively by a simple choice rule built into the human mind: pick the alternative with the highest payoff.[16]

Every day, we see people moving about, doing an enormous assortment of complicated tasks with seemingly uninterrupted orderliness; only rarely do we see disorder. Attributing such order to the political state mistakenly assigns causality where there is only concurrence. The state only exists at the expense of the working, cooperative members of society, while disrupting and prolonging their natural proclivity to orderliness.

We cannot expect order to emerge from the state's issuance of laws and rules that are too complicated to understand and too numerous to track. As complexity theory clearly shows, the application of simple, local rules produces orderly systems. With this new science, we can better understand why top-down, state-enforced plans to benefit society have failed and why any other plan — no matter how brilliant — will fail as well.

In *Complex Adaptive Systems,* John Miller and Scott Page suggest applying "keep it simple, stupid" (KISS) to the formulation of rules to bring about order. Scientific modeling seeks to find the simplest rule by removing all the unneeded

---

[16]Leda Cosmides and John Tooby, "Evolutionary Psychology, Moral Heuristics, and the Law," in *Heuristics and the Law*, edited by Gerd Gigerenzer and Christoph Engel (Cambridge, MA: MIT Press, 2006).

parts. Modeling is like stone carving: the art is in removing what you don't need.[17]

In *The Social Order of the Underworld*, David Skarbek illustrates how convicts develop their own rules of conduct that become far more effective in maintaining order than top-down prison rules. Prison guards rely on such self-imposed arrangements to govern affairs and adjudicate disputes between them.[18] If hardened criminals were isolated on a remote island without rules or guards, contrary to expectations, rules of conduct would emerge to govern their behavior. They would enforce contracts and recognize property rights. The ability of prisoners to defy prison authorities and live by their own rules of conduct has led to the adage, "The cons run the joint." In "running the joint," inmates construct a society unto itself and establish their own moral order.[19] Such a bottom-up emerging order belies Hobbes's grim view of man's state of nature.

I am always awestruck when I watch the hundreds of couples walking about in a shopping center and wonder how in the world all those people were able to find each other. There's no State Matchmaker Commission that regulates their activity to ensure adequate propagation; it happens spontaneously in a system where no one is obligated to satisfy the innate mating drive of another. Simple tit-for-tat local rules get the job done with little effort (arguably!). As Steven Pinker observes, people shop for the most desirable

---

[17]John H. Miller and Scott E. Page, *Complex Adaptive Systems: An Introduction to Computational Models of Social Life* (Princeton, NJ: Princeton University Press, 2007), p. 246.

[18]David Skarbek, *The Social Order of the Underworld, How Prison Gangs Govern the American Penal System* (Oxford University Press, 2014). Skarbek discussed his book during the IFREE/ESI Lecture Series at Chapman University on September 12, 2014, available at https://vimeo.com/107054811. See also Michael P. Marks, *The Prison as Metaphor: Reimagining International Relations* (New York: Peter Lang International Academic Publishers, 2004), ch. 5.

[19]Charles Stastny and Gabrielle Tyrnauer, "Applied: Who Rules the Joint?," *American Anthropologist* 85, no. 3 (1983): 716–17.

person who will accept them, and that is why most marriages pair a bride and a groom of roughly equal desirability. The tens marry tens, the nines marry nines, and so on. That is exactly what should happen in a marketplace, where you want the best price you can get (the other person) for the goods you are offering (you).[20]

Political intrusions into the volitional interaction of individuals minding their own affairs are no different from any other intrusions. Individuals adapt and adjust their actions accordingly to survive and prosper using the same cooperating/competing/ostracizing local rules that facilitated the survival of their ancestors. The greater the intrusion, the greater the effort individuals will make to search for and discover avenues and actions that diminish the impact.

The notion that forced compliance with rules imposed by political rulers supersedes one's volitional compliance with local rules will likely have fewer advocates as the new science of chaos, complexity, and self-organizing systems of nature works its way into general academic curricula. It is more likely that the political state will unravel faster than the academic community will assimilate into its curricula the reasons why such unraveling was inevitable.

The *idea* that a ruler can override the laws of nature is all that has ever existed because the actual ability to do so is illusory. The laws of nature are no more subject to the dictates of a king, senator, congressman, or bureaucrat today than they have ever been. Nevertheless, those trapped in the political box continue to harbor the mythical belief that political rulers can somehow defy the laws of nature by forcing people to be orderly and prosperous. Such idolatry is bewildering in a world where the historical track record of political intrusion is filled with the devastation of human populations in the hundreds of millions.

---

[20]Steven Pinker, "Crazy Love," *Time*, January 17, 2008, http://content.time.com/time/magazine/article/0,9171,1704692,00.html.

The massive edifice of the state is a clear indication of its inability to mastermind and engineer the interactions of individual members of society. The average annual issuance of more than seventy-five thousand pages of new proposed and final federal regulations from 2003 to 2016,[21] as well as new regulations issued by regional states, attests to the fact that their individual subjects are far more creative and imaginative than are those trying to rule them.

In his course "Great Scientific Ideas That Changed the World," Professor Steven Goldman states, "This complex multifaceted idea of systems theory, complexity/chaos theory, and self-organization theory is one of the greatest scientific ideas of all time and is revolutionizing what we mean by scientific knowledge."[22]

Evolution of living matter did not come about by a plan or with a discernible purpose; the interaction of a half-dozen common elements led to replicating matter called life. After some three to four billion years, here we are with brains capable of thinking about the entire process. I'm in awe (an understatement to be sure!) to think that my 185 millionth great-grandfather and great-grandmother were fish, but there they were, swimming around someplace on this planet with nary a thought of having me as their 185 millionth great-grandson. Natural evolution is a miraculous process that Richard Dawkins graphically captures in his book *The Magic of Reality*[23] and which Matt Ridley explores in *The Evolution of Everything*.[24]

---

[21]Clyde Wayne Crews Jr., *Ten Thousand Commandments, An Annual Snapshot of the Federal Regulatory State,* 2017 ed. Competitive Enterprise Institute, https://cei.org/10KC/Chapter-2.

[22]Steven Goldman, *Great Ideas That Changed the World* (The Teaching Company) Lecture 34, "System, Chaos and Self Organization."

[23]Richard Dawkins, *The Magic of Reality: How We Know What's Really True* (Free Press, 2012).

[24]Matt Ridley, *The Evolution of Everything: How New Ideas Emerge* (New York: Harper Perennial, 2016).

Leonard Read's masterpiece *I, Pencil: My Family Tree* depicts the beautiful essence of the invisible hand from which a miraculous pencil emerges. From thousands of individuals, independent of the others, each freely pursuing his own well-being, emerges a pencil — which no single person knows how to produce — to be used by a writer who doesn't know or give a thought to how it came to be.

The emergence of a pencil rests upon the same natural, bottom-up process as does the emergence of roads, eyes, education, trees, cities, justice, and rules. From the interaction of genes, cells, and individuals, unimaginable miracles emerge. Good economics is simply getting out of the way of miracle makers. As Leslie Orgel observed, "Evolution is smarter than you are." In time, economists will come to realize that a planned economy — no matter how skillfully designed — cannot result in the outcome for which it is designed. Everything naturally evolves.

As the political state's edifice unravels, humans will continue to interact and adapt, using simple local rules they heuristically discover as their guide for surviving and propagating. This new science of chaos and complexity is giving us invaluable insight into that process, while leaving us with the wonderment of an unpredictable outcome.

9

Political Democracy

The way you see people is the way you treat them, and the way you treat them is what they become.

— Johann Wolfgang von Goethe (1749–1832)

The urge to save humanity is almost always a false front for the urge to rule.

— H. L. Mencken (1880–1956)

Goodness in man can only grow in a climate of liberty.

— F.A. Harper (1905–1973)

LIBERTY IS A CONCEPT OF non subordination that those who embrace politics find most difficult to accept because without subordination political governments would not exist. Regardless of their titles, all political structures begin with the presumption of subordination. Classifying people into rulers and subjects is a prerequisite to the Constitution. Absent such classification, the rules of conduct would apply equally to everyone. As discussed throughout, government brings out the worst in people by granting constitutional immunity to acts by ruling members that are deemed criminal when done by others.

There are those in politics — even those claiming to be libertarians — who believe in the necessity of government, provided its power to rule is limited. They claim the Constitution grants the federal government the rightful authority to rule but contend it has abused its authority and power. The government is authorized to levy taxes, impose tariffs, wage wars, commandeer warriors, print money, prohibit trade, seize private property, and grant immunities and privileges. To contend that an abuse of power occurs only when these authorized activities exceed some arbitrary limit is a tortuous stretch of reasoning. To endorse such authorized powers even at a minimal level is to disavow any meaningful concept of liberty. Liberty is *not* something to be doled out by, or subject to, a superior authority, because the very notion of a person of such superiority is that mythical artifact libertarians find troublesome. Thomas Paine succinctly expresses this notion in *Common Sense*: "There is another and greater distinction for which no truly natural or religious reason can be assigned, and that is, the distinction of men into KINGS and SUBJECTS."

Justifying the legitimacy of a government based on the authority conferred on it by a proclamation authored by a few self-appointed individuals is spurious, regardless of their best intentions. The Constitution has no more authority to proclaim a superior ruling class than a king's proclamation that his authority to rule is God-given or a similar notion proclaimed by a few of my friends and me.

Defending the Constitution as a vehicle to curtail state intrusions into people's lives certainly cannot be based on its efficacy to do so. Once the Constitution was ratified, federal intrusions followed almost immediately, with expansions limited only by the time required to shepherd them through the constitutional political maze. As early as 1798, when the Constitution was only nine years old, the government passed the Alien and Sedition Acts, which, among other things, prohibited speech critical of the federal government.

One need only scan an issue of the *Wall Street Journal* or any other major newspaper and tally the articles covering state intrusions into citizens' peaceful affairs to recognize the Constitution's ineffectiveness as a means to curtail such intrusions.

Those enamored with government claim that roads, schools, defense, laws, and justice would not exist without it. Absent government, some claim wages would be pitiful, working conditions would be dismal, criminals would run loose, schools would disappear, women would be scorned, slavery would return, aliens would invade, air and water would be polluted, oceans would be depleted, the Earth would be scorched, food would be contaminated, and so on. According to Hobbes, without an all-powerful sovereign, humans would return to a state of nature, where life would be "solitary, poor, nasty, brutish, and short."[1] This allegedly necessary all-powerful sovereign has a historical record of hundreds of millions of lives cut short by famine and war, wherein every known form of brutality and nastiness has been used.[2]

When we envision the political state, we imagine an amorphous enigma, a kind of faceless "Uberman" that can miraculously defy nature by creating prosperity out of plunder, peace out of war, money by fiat, freedom out of mastery, and harmony out of divisiveness. Those who rely on such sorcery to bring about order and prosperity, regardless of who waves the magic wand, are destined to be disappointed because the actions taken are directly opposite to those that would naturally achieve the desired ends.

---

[1]Hobbes was an English philosopher and political theorist best known for his book *Leviathan* (1651). There, he argues that the only way to secure civil society is through universal submission to the absolute authority of a sovereign.

[2]Matthew White, *Atrocities: The 100 Deadliest Episodes in Human History* (W. W. Norton & Company, 2013).

The belief that there is a plan that if implemented will bring about a better society begs for someone with exceptional insight who knows the plan and can make it a reality. With that mindset, people open their door to every sort of political pundit claiming to be that messiah, ready and willing to implement his or her miraculous plan if given the chance. Political democracy encourages people to believe in the false notion that miraculous plans and political messiahs exist and in the equally false notion that dicta and force can bring about social order and a better society.

When confronted by the political mind with regard to how X would be provided or accomplished in the absence of government, the urge is strong to respond with descriptive ways X could be provided and accomplished. Yet, the more apt response, while not particularly satisfying, would be: "I can't know, since free markets don't come with blueprints." The political world is one of blueprints with myriad drafters and architects in constant debate, each with a notion of certitude. Thus, to suggest that the best solution is to scrap the blueprints would likely make for a very short debate! Those in the political world find such hands-off, bottom-up emergent workings too uncertain and slow. They are confident that their use of dicta and force can expedite a more peaceful and prosperous social outcome than that which emerges spontaneously from volition.

Nonetheless, whether by force or volition, we know that people — not the state — produce goods and services. Teachers educate, engineers build roads, financiers create financial markets, arbiters resolve disputes, guards provide protection, and physicians and nurses provide health care. These are real people. Yet they do not become more brilliant, energetic, efficient, moral, creative, or superhuman by way of the state. An abundance of facts shows that the very opposite is engendered in people at the hands of the state.

Politicians are masters at employing words and phrases that tell us what we want to hear while avoiding language that tells us what they are actually saying and doing. Companies such as Luntz Global use focus groups to evaluate the impact of words and phrases in political speeches. Its motto is "It's not what you say, it's what they hear." Founder Frank Luntz asserts, "My job is to look for the words that trigger the emotion."[3] Precise language can turn negative-sounding words into positive ones and vice versa. *Such sophistry is the art of politics.*

Underlying this sophistry, however, is the decaying stench of political democracy — most evident when a person can dictate with authoritative pride how others are allowed to conduct themselves in their most intimate relationships. Such a degrading and pompous display of inhumanity permeates every nook and cranny of human activity and exemplifies why political democracy brings out the very worst in people. The actual prohibitions that are adopted and enforced are the unavoidable symptoms of a political system wherein all human matters, no matter how intimate or innocuous, are subject to the dictates of a consensus.

To oppose a political policy on moral grounds but embrace the idea that a consensus is sufficient to rightfully enact it as law is to oppose a symptom while endorsing its cause. The idea that a political consensus is righteous has become so ubiquitous that most people today believe they are not only justified in sticking their nose into everyone else's business but also have a patriotic duty to do so. Political voting is a display of that belief, and to embrace such means to rule the lives of others is to believe in the same righteous fiction kings once employed. In each case, people are forced to behave at the pleasure of another. Whether people are forced to live at the pleasure of a tyrant or a political consensus, nature's feedback is indifferent. Using force to make people behave better will only make them behave worse!

---

[3]"Interview: Frank Luntz," *Frontline*, PBS, November 9, 2004, https://www.pbs.org/wgbh/pages/frontline/shows/persuaders/interviews/luntz.html.

Those who propose a mini-state to regain the degree of freedom Americans enjoyed when the nation was young and governed by a less intrusive government must envision a state based on an arrangement far different from that of the Constitution or a political democracy. Otherwise, such an arrangement, if attained, would simply revert to the same level of intrusion that now exists. In principle, a mini-state is no different from a maxi-state because the inherent nature of any state, regardless of size, is to forcibly prohibit individual secession — the very antithesis of freedom.

The Declaration of Covenants, Conditions, and Restrictions (CC&Rs) — whereby everyone in a given neighborhood agrees to a set of rules — is sometimes invoked to demonstrate the legitimacy of the state. An arrangement in which everyone in a community or neighborhood volitionally agrees to conduct themselves and maintain their property in a prescribed way is not incompatible with the concept of liberty. However, the alleged corollary of such a community to the state is foundationally invalid since one is founded on volition while the other is founded on force. The need for physical force in a political democracy implies that few people would buy or opt into the social arrangement volitionally.

The Constitution is not a set of rules agreed to by those who became subject to them. By eminent domain and without compensation, its authors simply commanded everyone residing within their claimed segment of the planet to obey their rules — like it or not. Libertarians who embrace liberty, freedom, personal responsibility, nonaggression, individualism, the Golden Rule, peace, and personal property while simultaneously embracing the Constitution must envision in each of those terms conditions that fall far afield from their general, everyday understanding.

In his popular book *The Righteous Mind: Why Good People Are Divided by Politics and Religion*, Jonathan Haidt claims that society would be better served if everyone understood why their political opponents think the way they do.[4] He sees those in the political world as primarily divided by their moral inclinations, not by reasoning. He identifies the moral inclinations of the left (liberals) as "caring and equality" and those of the right (conservatives) as "loyalty and justice." Haidt suggests that the better we understand the underlying moral instincts that drive our opponents, the more persuasive we will be in getting them to understand and appreciate our own views. He considers the use of reason and logic far less persuasive than appealing to people's emotions. Emotions certainly run high in the political world, where the more popular an opponent's views are, the more threatening they become to yours.

Regardless of a person's political leanings, it is the win/lose nature of the system that makes one so rabid about his or her views. When you are battling for things dear to your heart that someone else is trying to take away, it is difficult to think rationally. The ugliness of politics is not due to mere differences of opinion — it's the win/lose scenario that creates its ugliness. Outside the political world, people have myriad differences of opinions and preferences they can express without repressing the expression and preferences of others. The market seeks out every kind of expressed preference as an open invitation to provide satisfaction. You do not have to understand why someone's preferences are different from yours — you are simply thankful that they are. In contrast, the political world is a battlefield where you had better shoot down the other guy's preferences before he shoots down yours.

Haidt is concerned about the ugliness of politics. He believes the arena of the political world would become more civil if people were to step outside their "moral matrix," as he puts it. This moral matrix is not the instinctual moral compass that guides both liberals and conservatives. Neither group would likely advocate in their private

---

[4]Jonathan Haidt, *Righteous Mind: Why Good People are Divided by Politics and Religion* (New York: Vintage, 2013).

lives with friends, neighbors, and associates that which they advocate in their political lives for public affairs. Imagine a conservative forcing a neighbor to be loyal and just or a liberal forcing his neighbor to be caring and equal. The personal behaviors of liberals and conservatives are likely indistinguishable in their private affairs but completely at odds in the realm of political affairs.

People behave abhorrently in a political context because such conduct is the accepted norm. Sadly, Haidt is trying to cure what he sees as an ailment while embracing the disease. His claim that "hatred and mistrust damage democracy" is clearly backward. It is political democracy that damages respect and trust by pitting people against each other in a divisive frenzy for power that provokes hatred and mistrust.

If political democracy were as wonderful as many claim, the threat of physical force would not be needed to gain allegiance. Only this threat gives politicians an audience because without it, people would, for the most part, mind their own business. Without force, a political democracy would last but a few years because common sense, moral sentiment, reason, and secession would oblige politicians to find useful work, producing goods and services that people would buy volitionally.

It would be difficult to construct a more inhumane, demoralizing, and divisive social scheme than one based on political democracy, in which common sense and goodwill are scorned and individual predation is praised.

10

A Better Life — A Better World

What is important in life is life, and not the result of life.

— Johann Wolfgang von Goethe (1749–1832)

Be yourself; everyone else is already taken!

— Oscar Wilde (1854–1900)

To speak seriously: the standards of "goodness" which are generally recognised by public opinion are not those which are calculated to make the world a happier place. This is due to a variety of causes, of which the chief is tradition, and the next most powerful is the unjust power of dominant classes. We need a morality based upon love of life, upon pleasure in growth and positive achievement, not upon repression and prohibition. A man should be regarded as "good" if he is happy, expansive, generous and glad when others are happy; if so, a few peccadilloes should be regarded as of little importance. ... Reason may be a small force, but it is constant, and works always in one direction, while the forces of unreason destroy one another in

*futile strife. Therefore, every orgy of unreason
in the end strengthens the friends of reason, and
shows afresh that they are the only true friends
of humanity.*[1]

— Bertrand Russell (1872–1970)

WE HAVE AN INHERENT SENSE of deeds and duties — that is,
an underlying obligation to do good. At just about every
graduation ceremony I've attended (and probably mine
as well, but that was too long ago to recall), the graduates
are told to go out and change the world to make it a better place. Edmund Burke's statement (albeit apocryphal)
warns us that "all that is necessary for the triumph of evil
is that good men do nothing." Such statements are rallying
calls to action, and to snub your nose at such a call is seen
by many as antisocial or, worse, an endorsement of evil.

So you leave high school or college and go out into the
world — that "real" world you are told to change — and
ask yourself, "What do I actually do?" If you are going to
change the world for the better, you must identify what is
bad and make it good and find what is good and make it better. You look around and conclude that war, poverty, theft,
and cheating are bad and without them the world would
certainly be a better place. Where do you start, and again,
what do you actually do? You reason that the first thing you
can do about war is not to be in one. You certainly wouldn't
consider joining the military. The first thing you can do
about poverty is to work, avoid being poor, and possibly
start a business to help others avoid being poor. The first
thing you can do about theft and cheating is to refrain from
stealing, keep your word, and meet your obligations. After
you've accomplished all these "first things," you are somewhat pleased but not completely satisfied, and so you ask

---

[1]Bertrand Russell, "The Harm That Good Men Do," 1926, http://rus-
sell-j.com/0393HGMD.HTM.

yourself, "Now what? That was too simple. There must be more I can and should do to make the world a better place."

Eventually, you conclude that if everyone simply did the things you did and found to be so straightforward, the world would certainly be a far better place. You are *so* excited that you are itching to spread the word and get others excited about how they too can make the world a better place. Your recipe is clear and simple. You begin to proselytize. You talk and teach, and you attract a growing number of kindred followers. But the process is far too slow and life is too short. You are frustrated by the meager impact you're having on the world. You see others gaining notoriety, getting their ideas debated and laws passed. You know your ideas about how to make the world a better place are far better. In fact, you're not too keen on most of the other ways being proposed, and you're convinced some of them will even make the world worse. Yet no one is talking about you and your ideas except your friends, who like your ideas so much they encourage you to get into politics, where you can do more good by enacting your ideas into law.

What I've tried to capture here very loosely stems from the life of my dear friend Harry Browne, who authored several books, my favorite being *How I Found Freedom in an Unfree World*. Harry, who despised the state, was a great inspiration. Later in life, however, he became so disheartened about the direction the country was taking that he succumbed to the temptation of trying to fix it by getting into politics. I remember the day he called to tell me he had decided to run for president as the Libertarian Party candidate in the 1996 election.

"Why?" I asked with absolute shock and disappointment.

He responded, "The country is going to hell, and I can't take it any longer."

The sadness in his voice left me speechless and unwilling to try to convince him otherwise. He won the nomination and garnered the number of votes typical for a Libertarian candidate. Yes, the political stage is a difficult arena to avoid. I met and spoke with Harry several times during his campaign but never had the gumption to question his decision again. He died in 2006 and left me with the memorable lesson that those who want to do good are not always satisfied with just living their lives and minding their own business. I cannot question one's urge to get into politics to do good; I can only question how it is ever possible to do good by way of politics.

Many have been conditioned to believe that not participating in the political process is shameful and unpatriotic, especially when it comes to war. Political charlatans instill guilt in those unwilling to kill as a patriotic duty. State advertisements entice impressionable young men to fight wars by portraying military life as glorious and honorable. But the state would not dare show the sequel: a scene where you are blowing the head off a young man from a distant land or worse, getting your own head blown off. How sad to see a mother at a military burial service for her son receiving a folded flag as a badge of honor. No patriotic pride or honor in a mother's heart will overcome that sorrow.

Some may scorn the passive behavior of those who simply mind their own business as cowardly. Such passivity, however, does not mean they are wallflowers, since there's a great difference between pushing people away and pushing them around. Maybe the foremost way to make the world better is simply this: don't go to war, don't be on the dole, don't endorse politics, do good work, and mind your own business. This simple path to a better world may not be newsworthy or codified in history books, but it will give you the pleasure of living *your* life *your* way, knowing you didn't get in the way of others trying to do the same.

Index